S

and

Finish Well

The 7 Simple Components of a Meaningful Life

DIANE R. BUTTON

Better World Publishing
P.O. Box 455
Haleiwa, HI 96712

Editor: Hannah Button
Cover & Interior Design & Composition: Ehukai Marketing
Available to book sellers, online retailers, academic institutions
and libraries through Ingram Content Group.
Available Internationally on Amazon European websites.

Library of Congress Cataloging-in-Publication Data
    Button, Diane, 1959–
    Show Up and Finish Well – *The 7 Simple Components of a
    Meaningful Life* / Diane Button. p. cm.
    BISAC: Body, Mind & Spirit / Inspiration & Personal
    Growth

The corporate mission of Better World Publishing is: *Inspiring
lives of passion and service for a better world.*

FIRST EDITION
Copyright © 2016 Diane Button
All rights reserved.
ISBN-13: 978-1536871135
ISBN-10: 1536871133

DEDICATION

To all who courageously and lovingly showed up
and finished well.

And to my family…

Mark, you are my strength and goodness.
Carly, you are my courage and reflection.
Jack, you are my wisdom and depth.
Hannah, you are my curiosity and joy.

CONTENTS

INTRODUCTION

Showing Up

It was springtime. I was holding my grandfather in my arms when he died. The windows were open and there was a cool breeze blowing in his bedroom. His eyes closed and there was a warm smile of contentment on his face. At that very moment the church bells rang and echoed a sweet melody in the room. He had lived in peace and he died in peace.

It was that day I first became curious about finding meaning in my own life. I wished I had asked my grandfather more questions while he was alive. He lived an authentic life, filled with love and humility, and he died with a pure sense of integrity, contentment and fulfillment. My grandfather was one of the first plastic surgeons in America to do live skin

1

grafts on severe burn victims. I know he witnessed some of the worst pain a person could endure and he felt burdened by the loss of the lives he was unable save. He had his own hardships in life, too, beginning with the loss of both his parents when he was only four years old. Throughout his life he was very intentional, aware, and accepting, and he seemed to possess a wisdom that surpassed his intellectual knowledge and everyday understanding of life. It was as if he died with a secret that I never knew.

This book is not about dying. It is about showing up for life with all your heart and living well with a deep sense of meaning and purpose. It is about common threads, feelings and needs that we all share as human beings, not just for the final stages of life, but for living every day. And it is about finishing well, which means always knowing that you gave your whole self, and your best self, in all circumstances. It matters that we show up for the moments of our lives, the years of our lives, and the end of our lives. You have to show up in order to finish well.

It is my goal to share some lessons learned from my life, from my journeys with breast cancer and hospice work, and from the research collected during my master's thesis entitled, "The Seven Components of a Meaningful Life." My hope is for everyone I love to reach the end of their life with the same sense of serenity that I believe my grandfather possessed, and

2

to feel the deep peace that allowed him to leave this world with a smile on his face.

Thank you all for shining your light so that I may see more clearly. I am blessed beyond measure.

Diane

Show Up and Finish Well

CHAPTER 1

My Three Seeds

Dear Children,

My fortune cookie said, "Hold people tightly and things loosely." That reminded me of my mom, your Grandma Rose. Grandma has a lot of wonderful qualities, but she is so darn suspicious of people that sometimes she won't relax and let good stuff happen. She's always worried and everywhere she goes she clutches her purse tightly under her right arm. I call this condition "Pursitis." Sometimes she walks into our house and doesn't put her purse down for half an hour or more, clutching it under her arm until I remind her that we are not bank robbers.

Perhaps I should give her my fortune cookie.

I don't know exactly why, but that darn cookie made me think for days about my life, my remaining years, and my mortality in a way I had never considered before. The fortune was about attachment, but also about showing up for life in a way that really matters. There is an intuitive seed planted in me that knows that now is the time to begin consolidating all that remains unsaid, all the golden nuggets that a big mama bear like me desires to unload on her unsuspecting cubs, just in case I never get the chance.

Speaking of planting seeds, today I was watching your dad in the yard, tending to his garden with gentle, loving care. It is simultaneously a simple and a complex task. I am struck with the thought that parenting is much like gardening. It, too, is simultaneously a simple and a complex task.

In my garden, I was not given bags and bags full of seeds to scatter about the yard hoping that some would grow and produce a bountiful amount of sweet fruit. No, I was not given a large bag of seeds. I was simply given three. Three tiny seeds. Three seeds for me to plant, and water, and nurture. Three seeds for me to protect when the rains fall down and life's storms cover the afternoon sun. Three seeds whose roots I will never fully see, but nevertheless I pray that they run deep and wide and strong enough to proudly and confidently stand on their own. Three beautiful seeds that stretch up every morning in gratitude for another glorious day. Three seeds that know they are safe in their garden while slowly and peacefully reaching towards the stars.

"My Three Seeds" – Hannah, Jack & Carly (2003)

You kids have taken every possible feeling and emotion known to mankind and stretched me to the farthest corners of my potential as a human being. You have brought out the best in me. You have brought out the worst in me. I'll never forget the time Jack said so lovingly, "Hey mom, what if we all find out that I am actually the Baby Jesus and you are Mother Mary?" Yeah, right. Kids and their imaginations. I told him we probably didn't have to worry about that any time soon. The truth is, sometimes I think he really is a lot like Jesus...kind, compassionate and forgiving. I just don't have a lot in common with Mary.

Retrospectively, I have taken so much time nurturing, grooming and growing you up on the outside. There was the graduation from the bathtub to the shower, the teeth brushing, hair washing and then finally came the dreaded shaving! There was soccer, gymnastics, singing, acting, Model United Nations, drums, Ultimate Frisbee, the horse arena, Math League, community service and more. There was the room cleaning, dish washing, toilet scrubbing, car washing and finally a bit of laundry training before college. And let's not forget learning to drive, dating, the SAT prep, and the college application process. Countless hours spent navigating through what at the time seemed to be so urgent, so relentlessly necessary.

This is about none of that.

This is about living life from the inside out.

And it is infinitely more important.

Why has it taken me so long to get here? It has always been clear to me that you each have your own journey to complete here on earth. I am simply a coach, a cheerleader, and finally the one who passes the baton and watches you sprint for that final lap of your own. And you have shined. There is so much more to life than clean laundry and sparkly teeth. There is inner strength, and character. There is integrity and tolerance, mixed with a healthy worldview. There is reflection and curiosity and there is a thirst for knowledge and education that breaks through the barriers of traditional learning.

Oh, it has not been without its challenges, especially during those teenage years when, according to you, I lost half my I.Q. and, on occasion, all of my patience. Nonetheless, I am proud. And grateful. You are showing up for your life, 100%.

So now it is time for me to begin to let go, sit back with a big smile on my aging face and watch you venture out on your own into this crazy, complicated world. But wait! Not so fast! There are too many life lessons to learn, too many unspoken words. Yes, you can cook a turkey and burp the alphabet, but do you know the secret ingredients for a meaningful life?

In case I am not here to share "The Seven Simple Components of a Meaningful Life" with you over the years, let this project be my legacy of love for you all. You are the greatest joys I have ever known in this life, and I don't want to miss any of the milestones yet to come. But if God takes me from this earth, then I will find peace in knowing that I have shared my entire heart with you.

From a spiritual perspective, that is not entirely true. I believe I will find lasting peace in eternity whether I share my heart or not. Yes, I will be dead, but I will also be free from the trappings of cellulite and random, unwanted hairs and I will be dancing with the angels. So, this legacy is for you, and for those I love and am leaving behind. It is my heart. All of it. After a lifetime of writing letters for you to open on special milestones in your life, consider this the final letter in your Letter Box.

When I was a teenager, I began writing down notes, quotes, thoughts and tidbits of wisdom. I wrote them constantly…in books, on note cards, on ripped pieces of paper and sometimes on my left arm. I wrote them on my bedroom wall, hung them on posters and wrote songs and poems about them. Sometimes something profound or funny would happen and I would write those stories down, too.

Over the past few years I have gathered my notes, which were literally scattered across the country, from Hawaii to Tennessee. Because there are too many to tattoo all over my body, I am presenting them here, along with my research about a meaningful life, in the hopes that, at a young age, you begin to understand the simplicity of life and love. Perhaps you will learn to love and accept yourself wholeheartedly. Perhaps you will sing louder and laugh more. And, please, on top of everything, be gentle with yourself. The ride will be less bumpy that way.

May you live in truth, authenticity and peace,

Mom

Show Up and Finish Well

CHAPTER 2

The 7 Components of a Meaningful Life

My research has unveiled seven common threads which are shared by those who have come to the latter part of their life, and who feel that they have lived a life of deep meaning and purpose. Regardless of race, religion, wealth, fame or social status, these people have created a life that matters to others and, most importantly, to themselves. They have all struggled, yet the struggles were met with courage and considered a holy walk through the darkness. They sought and found hope in the smallest sliver of light. They embraced joy, and seemed to understand that the good times come and go, and the hard times do, too. They know that joy comes from each sacred moment that God has given to them, and they know without a doubt that the moment to live fully and authentically is now.

Most of my lifetime collection of notes and short stories fit into at least one of these seven components of a meaningful life. We seek these aspects of our being on a subconscious level, which is why most of my notes, even as a teenager, centered around a yearning for purpose and meaning. And a yearning to belong. And a yearning to make my life matter. But the truth is, we can stop searching because everything we need is already here. I'm advocating for a lifetime of discovery and living well, rather than a lifetime of searching.

I will include the data and research findings from my thesis and interviews in the rest of this book, but for now, here is a glimpse into the tapestry of our inner journeys. My hope is that you will incorporate some or all of these into your daily life, building a life of meaning from this moment until the day you take your final breath. All you need to do is be willing to show up with your whole heart.

Showing Up with Gratitude – Giving thanks and expressing gratitude for the good times as well as the challenges, which provide an opportunity for us to grow and smooth our edges.

Showing Up with Intention – Living in a purposeful and thoughtful way, which includes making plans, having goals, knowing what brings you joy, knowing your passions, and acting upon them, and making responsible choices about relationships, careers and health.

Showing Up with Faith and Spirituality – Incorporating faith and spirituality into everyday life as a conscious decision, whatever that may mean for you.

Showing Up with Acceptance – Including acceptance of yourself, the people in your life, and the people on the planet as a whole. This also includes accepting the circumstances of your life, which in turn gives you the power to change them if you want or need to.

Showing Up with a Positive Attitude – Fostering a positive attitude by being optimistic, focusing on the good, being kind, and choosing activities and making life choices that bring joy, contentment and peace whenever possible.

Showing Up with Love and Relationships – Giving and receiving love, building deep, honest relationships, and practicing the dynamics of love for all of mankind and all of life. Love wins.

Showing Up with Charity and Contribution –
Making a selfless contribution to the planet, or to the people in it. Even one small act of compassion or kindness will leave the world a better place.

The time to show up, to build a life, to heal relationships, to love well and to take risks, is not later…it is now. If you wait until you are done with what you are doing now, you have missed the point entirely. And you may have missed an opportunity as well.

We want relationships. We want love and truth and laughter. And when we feel truly loved, we are loved for who we are, flaws and all. You are more than enough, just the way you are! You are a living, breathing soul, linked together with all of humanity. And you belong here, because your unique soul is the fingerprint of God on this earth.

My hope is that I can share with you these seven components that create the tapestry for a meaningful life so that you can start weaving them together now for your own life. Having meaning in your life is exhilarating. And, with awareness, a meaningful life is simple and achievable for all of us.

be still

Searching for Significance

What is a good life? Or a successful life? Or a meaningful life? We hear so often, "I just want to be happy" but what exactly does that look like and how will we know when we have arrived? Oh, and then, how do we stay there? A few years ago as part of my masters research project, I completed a phenomenological study of senior adults. A simple way of saying this is that I was privileged to interview people who have lived long enough to tell me how they came to a place where their lives felt both joyful and meaningful. The results of my probing and interviewing are detailed throughout these pages, and a few things are perfectly clear. There are definitely seven key common threads among those who feel their lives have been meaningful, but first, some other facts to keep in mind:

1. No one is holding on to hundred dollar bills when they die. Actually money has little to nothing to do with joy and happiness.

2. A simple life can be a deeply meaningful life. Simplicity may include quiet time, whole foods, deep conversations, sleep and less material possessions.

3. Meaning varies from person to person and it is up to each of us to find our own path. You are unique and just as God created you to be.

17

4. In generations past, meaning was handed down through traditions, family ties, and the trades. Survival was the root motivation for choices, with each person contributing their skills and knowledge in a collectivist society. Today, in the Western world, the separation of our individualistic society can be lonely.

5. We may travel a million miles in our lifetime, but the richest journey of life is the journey inward. It is simple to explain but more complicated to understand. Nothing external or physical will bring us closer to the divine or fill us with a peace that passes all understanding. It all comes from within.

6. We need to cuddle more, touch more, sing more songs together and unplug. If life is really about people and humanity, then why are so many of us choosing an electronic device as our primary relationship? A laptop cannot hug you back.

7. Just the fact that you are alive means that your life is meaningful. You matter to others and you have made a difference, even if you just smiled at a stranger. Embrace that!

be still

I'm So Busy

Let this be a challenge to NEVER answer the question "How are you?" with either of the two over-used and automatic answers, "I'm so busy" or "fine."

I freely admit that I am guilty of using those auto-responses repeatedly, but I literally cringe every time I say either of them. To me, it's dismissive and a way to avoid intimacy. Sometimes, for example, when you are checking out at the grocery store or talking to the United Airlines ticket agent, the word "fine" is easy and just keeps the conversation rolling because you assume they really don't want to know how you are actually doing. So we say we are fine even if we are going to a funeral, in serious pain, or just lost our job. Imagine how the United Airlines ticket agent would respond if she asked, "How are you today?" and you answered by telling her that you were feeling sad because your cat was just hit by a car, or you are scared because you need a surgery and don't have health insurance.

When someone who truly cares about you says, "How are you?" the absolute worst of all answers is "fine." How boring and untrue is that response? Who is fine anyway? And we all know that "fine" means something between "F'd up, Insecure, Neurotic and Evasive" or the more eloquent

"<u>F</u>eelings <u>I</u>nside <u>N</u>ot <u>E</u>xpressed." No one is ever just fine. Life is so much more intriguing than that.

But "I'm so busy" comes in second place and for some reason gets under my skin even more than when my husband talks and crunches on ice at the same time. We wear our "busy-ness" like a badge of honor or a symbol of self-importance. Since when did being busy become such a popular and cool thing to be?

Why glorify being busy? What about when families got up at 4:00am to milk cows and hurl manure? Are we busier than they were? And what are we so busy doing? Things we hate, or things we love?

Instead, set a goal to answer the question with some depth, some insightful probe into your mood and feelings. Next time someone asks, "How are you?" take a moment and actually tell them. Besides, lots of times we are feeling much better than fine, and either way, it's an opportunity to pause and check in with yourself. Are you hungry, thirsty or tired? Are you excited, worried, relaxed, peaceful, filled with energy, joyful, nervous, or calm? People who love you want to know!

I learned how to slow down and stop being so busy the hard way. Nobody would want cancer. Yet many will say, after they have been through treatment and are on the road to recovery, that they would not trade their path or change their story if they could. Some will say that cancer was a gift. That's cliché but exactly how I feel. Cancer changed my entire family. It opened all of our hearts to generosity, kindness and a desire to help others. We became a little less busy and a little more loving, more simple, and even a little more patient.

"Just an Ordinary Day"

From My Cancer Journal:

It's been three days since I had chemo and I have spent most of the day in bed feeling sick, which is not my idea of a very exciting, fun or romantic Valentine's Day. Mark sat by my side and worked on his laptop all day. It was all rather uneventful, actually. Just an ordinary day…like so many days lately that have been spent just waiting for time to pass, waiting for pain to subside, waiting to be done with chemo, waiting to heal.

I'm impatient for life to get back on track, but I wonder why? It is clear that my life will never be "back on track" and I would never want that life back anyway. It occurred to me this morning that all my life I have sought out so much on the outside: excitement, success, pleasure, fun, happiness, beauty, as if every day needed to be a spectacular improvement upon the one before. Never a dull moment… I never wanted just an ordinary day.

Today I see a different picture: family, friends, faith, love, acceptance, gratitude, and peace. I've been feeling a lot of those good inside feelings through this time. More and more, there is an unexplainable calm within this chaos called cancer. I have lost most of my desire for spectacular fireworks, success, beauty, notoriety, or wealth that seeks extreme proportions. It's simple now. What I long for is a conversation with the kids in the morning over a bowl of oatmeal and the sounds of laughter and singing in the house. I want to brush Hannah's hair, watch Jack do a flip, listen to Carly as she reads me her latest poem and then be greeted with a big hug from Mark when he comes home at the end of the day. Why did it always have to be so hard? Why has it taken so long?

Why is it that I never knew before that all I really wanted was just another ordinary day?

CHAPTER 3

Showing Up with Gratitude

Dear Cancer,

Thank you. You came early to the party, so I apologize for not being a gracious hostess.

Dear Heartbreak,

Thank you. You allowed me to change dance partners in the middle of a song.

Dear Suffering,

Thank you. Your darkness made the twinkle lights shine like the midnight sky on a moonless night.

Dear Death,

Although we have not met, I shall see you someday.

I trust you will arrive in time to gently caress my tender soul as I bid farewell to an unforgettable evening.

~ Diane R. Button

The Research About Gratitude

Gratitude comes from a heart that possesses a desire to show thankfulness or appreciation. It is a combination of an emotion and a state of being, and is usually accompanied by a verbal or physical action. When we are grateful, we are often motivated to thank someone, hug someone, or share our full heart, which is a positive feeling. Acclaimed U.C. Davis professor Robert Emmons is a pioneer in the emerging field of positive psychology and has spent more than a decade studying gratitude. He is the author of *Thanks! How the New Science of Gratitude Can Make You Happier.* Emmons teaches that when we practice thankfulness and gratitude, it is a means of expressing the fact that we are aware of the goodness we have received in our lives. He has linked gratitude with a long list of health-related benefits including stronger immune systems, lower blood pressure, more feelings of joy, more connection to others and an overall greater sense of well-being.

Many spiritual practices believe that human beings are born with everything they need to be genuinely happy, content, and peaceful in life. The missing ingredient for many people is the awareness of all that they have.

Many famous people throughout history have practiced gratitude including Mother Teresa, Martin

Luther King, Jr., Mahatma Gandhi, Albert Einstein, Carl Jung, the Dalai Lama, Oprah Winfrey, Deepak Chopra, Maya Angelou, Shakespeare, Leonardo Da Vinci, Sheryl Crow, Clint Eastwood, Jerry Seinfeld, Francis Ford Coppola, Seth MacFarlane, and Alicia Keys. The list goes on and on.

Even Jesus, the Son of God and Creator of the Universe, practiced gratitude for the goodness in his life. He thanked God for answered prayer. He stopped and expressed thanks to God for the food he received as a blessing before he ate and drank. We read in the Bible that Jesus said thank you for the food he multiplied so that others could eat and also at the Last Supper. In fact, over half of Jesus' public prayers were specific prayers of thanksgiving.

Counting your blessings, both large and small, is most often a path towards joy and a full and abundant heart. A mindset of thanksgiving can uproot negativity and unhealthy thoughts. Being aware of the goodness in your life, and even verbalizing or writing down why these are blessings for you, helps you see what you have rather than what you don't. And from there, we often realize that what we have is enough, or even more than enough.

In every interview I conducted for my thesis, whether formal or informal, gratitude was a theme woven throughout all aspects of people's lives. Many expressed gratitude for their parents for being supportive and a positive influence. Even those who expressed negative childhood memories and experiences were able to express gratitude for the lessons they learned from those circumstances. Many have endured pain and heartache, yet through that they learned how to love and raise healthy children despite their upbringing. They may not forget, but they are survivors, and for this they are grateful.

Specifically, people felt gratitude for their health, careers, spouses, family and friends, their knowledge, their passions and for the foundation their parents gave them as children. But there is another common thread, and that is gratitude for the simple things, the seemingly small things. It is this everyday awareness of all that is good that builds a grateful life.

Show Up and Finish Well

Stories About Gratitude

God Is Yellow

I am not the type of person who gets up at 4:00am to pray or meditate. I don't always remember to pray before meals or at bedtime, either. I also don't like to pray anywhere where people gather to pray together. I just feel awkward and weird about that, like everyone is thinking, "Wow, her prayers are strange." Or, "I wonder if she thought about that prayer in advance," as if I keep a list of possible prayers in my back pocket. So, that pretty much rules out church, too.

Yet, I seem to pray a lot.

Why? Because I try to do my best to pray and thank God for the gift of life itself every time I see the color yellow. Like God, yellow is everywhere. It's not brown like dirt, blue like sky or green like grass. Those colors are almost in every landscape you see. But yellow is different. Yellow is everywhere, you just have to look for it to truly see it. And even if you don't see it, it's still there. Just like God.

Because attitude and gratitude happen to rhyme, it's

somewhat melodic to say "an attitude of gratitude" but in reality, gratitude is so much more than an attitude. It is a way of life. It is a conscious choice we make. It is a practice that requires awareness and the ability to pause in appreciation or to find that still moment to say thank you.

One of my favorite parts of my life is the privilege of being a volunteer at Hospice. It is an honor to bear witness to the spirit of love that almost always fills the home of a dying person. People ask how I can handle being around sadness and death, but I find it beautiful. Aside from the fact that it is an inevitable transition that we all will experience some day, it is also pure, real, honest and deep. I see more kindness when I am with families in hospice care than at any other time of my life.

The Eyes of Gratitude

From my hospice journal:

Today I bathed three dying men. Fred was the first and he is a kind and gentle soul. He is simple and innocent, like a baby. He gently relaxes and allows me to care for him. He does not speak, but I can see the gratitude in his eyes.

Next I went to see Henry, who has been slowing

down over the past five weeks, but really declining these past few days. He asks for a back rub and I am honored. It occurs to me that this may be the last time someone rubs his back. So I take my time and make sure that he knows that, for this sweet time, he is all that matters to me. He smiles at me, and slowly lifts his hand over his heart, and I see the gratitude in his eyes.

Then there's Ralph. Last week Ralph was shouting out and angry. Today he is peaceful and calm. Everything about him seems slower and he has stopped eating solid foods. But he loves strawberry ice cream, and I get to feed him a giant bowl with pieces of fresh strawberries. I try to make each spoonful just perfect. He savors every bite, staring into my eyes the entire time. When he is finished, he whispers a soft, sweet "thank you" and he smiles. But he didn't have to, because I already saw the gratitude in his eyes.

be still

I used to always be asking God for something…and often it was something shallow and meaningless. "Dear God, please help me get a new, shiny sports car. Dear God, please let the flight be empty so I can get upgraded to first class. Dear God, please give 15 pounds of my fat to Suzie, that skinny bitch who lives on the corner. Dear God, I want I want I want."

I have learned that when I am silent, like in meditation or a rare moment of stillness, God speaks to me. But if I am busy talking all the time trying to get my shallow needs met, then how am I ever going to be able to hear the voice of God. So now, if I have anything at all to say to God, it is usually just a simple prayer. I just say, "thank you."

When I go to my yoga meditation class, taught by my friend Collette, she often does something of a spiritual "body scan." I try really hard to pay attention as we lay in silence on the floor and slowly go through all the parts of our body. I think the idea is to honor and pay attention to each body part. And in everyday life, I rarely take the time to acknowledge all that my right elbow has done for me in my life. Or all the joy that my earlobes have brought to my wardrobe and me. So, for this brief time, I focus in on each and every part of me.

The problem is that my mind often drifts away. I finally realized this when Collette said, "Right thumb, second finger, third finger, fourth finger, fifth finger," and then I would be on my own mental track and think, "sixth finger, seventh finger…"

So, I changed how I listen to the body scan, and every time Collette says, "right knee" I respond,

"Thank you, God, for my right knee."

Our bodies truly are miraculous. They are complex beyond imagination, our skin and bones, and organs and blood and everything that works together so perfectly over our lifetimes to get us through each day. Thank you to our bodies! Imagine how much our feet have done for us over the years! It is all a miracle.

It is a testament to the power of gratitude to try to be sad and grateful at the same time. If you allow yourself to sit with your sadness, and then shift away from your sadness to a heart filled with that which you are grateful for, even something seemingly small, your sadness will soften or even melt away. If you are in deep emotional or physical pain, searching for a sliver of gratitude may just give you a simple moment to catch your breath. It's a process and it works like this:

Our attitude comes from our thinking.

Once we change our thoughts,

It shifts our attitude.

Then we can begin to practice gratitude,

And gratitude comes from our heart.

And a whole, full heart leads us to joy,

And joy comes from our soul.

Someone told me once that it is impossible to smile when you are thinking a negative thought. I think the way it works is that you can't truly smile if you are *feeling* a negative thought. The thing about smiling, laughing, and being thankful is that you are focused on what you have that is positive. It increases your vitality and energy and lowers your stress. As a cancer survivor, lowering stress is important to me.

I made up my own exercise to make me smile if I'm feeling low. I just close my eyes, take a deep breath and start visualizing everything in my life that I am grateful for. The pictures from my life start appearing as if I am turning the pages of my memoir, slowly taking in all the goodness that has blessed my path through life... cuddling with my dog when I was a little girl, the red sunrise on a South African pier, dancing naked to Marvin Gaye in high school, the old man I spent the day salmon fishing with in the San Francisco Bay who showed me what true love looks like, baby pictures of each of my children, morning coffee with Cathy, the picture of me pregnant in Mexico with cellulite that my friend Reggie watched me tear into a thousand pieces,

Mark's voice when he says, "You're my girl," my bald head that survived cancer... and on and on. I am usually smiling after the first few and to me, that feels like gratitude.

We must be careful of anger, for anger is a robber of gratitude. Once I was really angry with an old boyfriend and I went to his house to confront him. When I walked in he was sleeping on the couch with his little puppy nestled in his arms. I instantly melted. The puppy was adorable, but a sleeping human is pretty adorable, too. That has become one of my favorite tools for overcoming anger. If I have ever been mad at you, then you can assume I have imagined you sleeping. Just try it. Think of one person who really pisses you off. And then, imagine them sleeping. It's just a little nugget, but I've just found that it's really hard to be mad at someone when you think of them all curled up in the fetal position like a little, innocent baby, like we all once were.

And if you imagine them sleeping all curled up and you are still totally pissed off, throw the cutest imaginary puppy into their arms and see if that helps. If not, well, then it may be time to move on. How's that for some cheap and instant gratification kind of therapy!

I Need You

Feeling gratitude is one thing, but expressing it is another. Express gratitude and appreciation whenever you get the chance! William Arthur Ward said, "Feeling gratitude and not expressing it is like wrapping a present and not giving it." A simple thank you can say so much. Thank you says, "I appreciate you. I like you. I acknowledge your time and effort. I value and respect you." Sometimes it even says, "I need you."

Throughout my life, my independence and stubbornness have kept me at arms length from feeling like I "need" someone. Even the word "need" when used in the context of another human being used to make me cringe. I need coffee. I need a vacation. I need exercise and probably some Botox. But the idea of needing another person had always felt weak and powerless to me. Then God rained on my imaginary parade of independence with a large malignant tumor. And I needed help. But then I realized that it was more than needing help. I needed people and support from them. Help comes from people, which meant that I had to tell my husband, "I need you."

It still makes me want to barf just a little when I say that, but it's true. When we are little babies, we need someone to meet all of our basic human needs. Even teenagers need their parents. Often, when we are old, we are like babies again and need to be cared for and to have someone help us with our daily needs.

But what about all those decades in the middle? We need each other then, too!

"MY" Glass Ball

"This year is going to suck," I lamented, just three days into the new year.

"Why do you say that?"

"I can just feel it."

"Well, then it's going to be a long year!"

I grabbed the dog and my friend, Peter, and headed out to the beach. A change of scenery was in order, as evidenced but my incredibly wicked attitude. There had been a tremendous storm the night before, and debris was scattered all over the beach. The normally peaceful and pristine beach was smelly and dirty. We stepped over rocks and piles of wood and my mood was getting even worse by the minute.

And then I saw it. Resting along the shoreline in a foamy mound of seawater was a beautiful, bright, turquoise glass ball. I picked it up and felt immediately like it had some magic power that was going to change the doomed fate of the remaining 362 days. There were barnacles and mussels hanging from the glass, but I could see the beauty glistening through the weathered façade.

"I'm keeping this," I said to Peter. I marched up the sand towards the house, gently nestled the glass ball safely into a billowy green shrub and set out to finish our walk on the deserted beach. The entire time we were there, only one person walked by.

On the way home, I ran up to the spot where the glass ball was hidden and discovered it was gone. Peter, not knowing that I really cared that much, said he thought he saw the one guy on the beach carrying it.

"Why didn't you tell me?" I asked Peter as if I would have chased him down for it.

For being in such a crappy mood, I thought my immediate reaction was really healthy. I realized it is just a "thing" and I'm not so into things anyway. And it was smelly, anyway. And maybe he will enjoy it more than I would. No big deal.

Until I got home.

It seems that EVERYONE in my neighborhood

knows and had to inform me in great detail that these glass "Japanese fishing balls" are supremely rare and valuable, over 40 years old, and "a collector's item." When I told my friend, Twila, she looked at me as if I had just lost the diamond off of my wedding ring.

All of a sudden, I felt like I had been robbed. Or like I had thrown away a winning lottery ticket. The damn glass ball, that I didn't even know about two hours before, was now occupying my every thought. The grief cycle comes to mind: Anger, sadness, bargaining. Acceptance was nowhere in sight. I was angry at this asshole who stole my glass ball! What a jerk. He saw my "markings" in the sand and followed the footprints to my secret spot and stole it!

Rationally, I know it is a public beach and if I was coveting this ball so much, I should have kept it with me. But apparently I didn't care enough until I learned of its supposed value.

Days later I was still consumed with thoughts of MY glass ball, although I noticed that my charge was fading and I was able to laugh a little bit at how stupidly attached I became to a "thing."

The next Saturday my friend, Kendra, and I went to the farmer's market. We bought our fresh, colorful, local vegetables, met friends, and listened to music. Somewhat spontaneously, we decided to inquire with the band about ukulele lessons. The band sent us down the road to a beautiful plantation-style house where they lived. Their mom greeted us and even invited us in. This was a vibrant family of artists and musicians and the house was alive with energy, color, and love. We all had one of those delightful conversations that bounced around from topic to topic, all inspiring and filled with joy, laughter and familiarity, like we were old friends from years past. Then somehow we got into the story of MY glass ball. And I was thinking about how some stories just have shitty endings.

We talked some more, and were finally getting ready to leave. My heart was filled with the joyful feeling you get when you are sharing life with kindred spirits and everything else has peeled away except the moment you are living right now.

As we were departing, the mom whispered something into her daughter's ear. When she returned, she handed me a glowing, beautiful turquoise Christmas ornament. It was MY new blue ball. I wanted to cry. It was so sweet of her, and the color was mesmerizing. I could see my face in the ornament.

But then this sweet mom said to her daughter, "No, that's not what I wanted." She stepped away for just a few seconds, and honestly I was a little disappointed because this was going to be a beautiful ending to my story and I would cherish it every Christmas. And now I thought she was going to take it away…again! Another lost blue ball. But soon she came back into the room and presented me with an amazing, beautiful, deep blue colored glass Japanese fishing ball that she had been saving for a long time.

She gently dropped it into my hands and said, "Now I know what I was supposed to do with this," as if she had been waiting for me to show up for years.

Kendra and I left, and I tightly wrapped the bright, blue Japanese fishing ball in my arms as we walked away. There were tears in my eyes and I was smiling in gratitude for such a happy ending.

be still

"Happy Thanksgiving!"

From my cancer journal:

My first chemo treatment made me feel anxious and somewhat scared, but so far I am well. It was an "unusual" experience to say the least. Yet, four days have passed and I am apparently still choosing to feel peaceful! The only really annoying symptom that I have right now is a constant nausea. For you moms, it's exactly like pregnancy nausea. Not the kind where you are really sick, the kind that lingers and just doesn't go away. So that's the chemo update...and still...today feels like THANKSGIVING!

Last week my friend Michelle called. She is going through chemo for breast cancer, too. She is younger than me, but is like a big sister right now. She drove us out on Natchez Trace to get out of the house and see the sun shining through the fall leaves. We took time to really look around and enjoyed every minute. We talked and laughed really hard about the weirdness of going bald, losing breasts and hair and all the other things that are shared by someone who can truly relate. That felt like the first day of real "Thanksgiving."

Our family has so much to be thankful for. I remember the first week I was diagnosed with cancer. Our neighbor and friend, Becky, came over to check on my and give me a giant hug. She asked me in her sweet Southern way, "Honey, who is in charge of your meals?" I had no idea what she was talking about...I am, of course. But she told me not to worry, that she was going to take care of us now and that we didn't need to worry about dinners during this time. I was stunned and found it hard to accept at first. So many people have brought us food. Yesterday, Becky came by with pies, vegetables, side dishes, homemade rolls and all kinds of delicious goodies for our Thanksgiving meal. Another day of "Thanksgiving."

One night the doorbell rang. I was in bed and Mark answered the door. He talked a bit to the woman who brought us food. We didn't even know her, yet she cooked us a meal. Why? We had no idea who she was or even how she knew us.

After she left, Mark came into the room and sat down on the bed next to me. He was emotional and could barely speak. "Why are you crying?" I asked.

Mark said, "I feel like Jesus just knocked on our door."

That is truly a servant's heart. From old friends who call to laugh and cry with us to people we don't even know, we learned that EVERY day is Thanksgiving.

I remember when I was younger and I thought I could change the world. One day I read a quote by Mother Teresa that encouraged all human beings to "do small things with great love." Small things. I liked that. But are they really small things?

Every week, our friend Nancy bakes us a loaf of sourdough bread. Every week. She bakes one for Michelle's family, too, and others I don't know. But that's what she does. She bakes us bread. For me, she is Mother Teresa. She is Jesus. She is who I want to be every day of my life. Because the truth is, it is not a small thing. For me, it is a huge thing. A simple loaf of bread, made with great love. It reminds me of why we're all here and, in a real sense, gives me hope.

CHAPTER 4

Showing Up with Intention

Rise up, young leaders.

For I am yesterday,
   And WE are today.

But YOU are tomorrow.

Tread thoughtfully as our ground
 has become unstable.

Be the one
   whose wisdom and actions
   are the rich, fertile soil...

The beginning
   of a perfect rose.

     ~ Diane R. Button

Show Up and Finish Well

The Research About Intention

Rabbi Harold Kushner spent decades writing books that offer guidance about living a life that matters. He sat with many people during the final stages of their lives, and he heard many stories about how people feel in their final days or hours. He encouraged young people in his congregation to ask themselves, "What kind of a person do I want to be?" He teaches that we are good people, and some have made poor choices in life, and that is because we are human. And often, people are still wrestling with the repercussions of those choices until the very moment of death.

Rabbi Kushner noted that those who despise old age or fear dying the most are those who feel they have not done anything worthwhile, and are not able to quiet the gnawing voice of disappointment. In his book, *Living a Life that Matters,* Rabbi Kushner writes, "It was not death that frightened them; it was insignificance, the fear that they would die and leave no mark on the world."

The word "intention" has become a key word in church sermons, motivational speeches and the recent movements towards positive psychology and health psychology. In the spiritual context, intentionality is akin to our free will and the application of our cognitive resources to make decisions that influence our lives and circumstances. Motivational speakers and professors often use the word "intention" to refer to setting goals, career planning and developing healthy habits or life skills.

In the humanistic model of psychology, which looks at the whole person, it is understood that humans are aware beings. They are also aware of their awareness. Humans make choices, assume responsibility and are intentional. Humans aim towards goals, and are aware that their decisions effect the future. They constantly seek meaning, value, and significance, even in everyday experiences. They are also usually aware that their choices will have consequences. Therefore, to live fully requires thoughtful intention.

In my research, I discovered that intention does not originate as a verb or even an action word. It is not only about being active or productive or checking things off on a long list of external life goals. Instead, intention begins as a sincere energy or an internal "knowing." It is a yearning from the soul. It is a heartfelt and genuine "yes" to something that personally matters. When an intention feels right, it resonates within you and sometimes tugs at you for years before you even notice or acknowledge that it is there. But when you see it, and feel it, you know it. Intention is like love at first sight. There are no wrong answers. There is no uncertainty. When you are prepared, strong and confident, there is also less fear. And then, when you are ready, the final step is to take action.

I have had the privilege of interviewing many people who feel they have lived intentional lives. Their stories are inspiring although most are not stories of earth-shattering fame, wealth or notoriety. While their desires and goals were widely varied, from being a stay at home mom to bike riding through the south of France to being part of the release of prisoners from a concentration camp in Dachau, their life decisions have been clearly thought through and articulated throughout the decades.

One of the key elements of intention, from my study, is the continual re-evaluation of life and subjective well-being. Just by honestly and purposefully checking in with themselves, people were able to identify points of time in their lives when they needed to make a change, or when they felt stagnant. At those times they took action when possible. They pursued new interests and they continued learning and engaging in new activities throughout their lives. Intention is not a destination, but a way of being.

My favorite common thread regarding intention, that percolates within all the people who have lived full and meaningful lives, is that they have all embraced life wholeheartedly and with the curiosity and enthusiasm of a child. The key factor is that every single one of them added something new to their lives at least every decade. They learned a language, began kayaking or biking or baking. They planted gardens, learned photography or did volunteer work, mentored a child, learned a musical instrument or started painting. They changed jobs and travelled and then built a canoe. They lived and they cultivated joy and they explored life.

Goals come from your brain, but intentions come from your heart.

Stories About Intention

Own Your Space

"Hit the Pause Button!" and "Own Your Space!" are two common sayings in our home. I'm sure it sounds dumb, but we all know what they mean. They are usually shouted with urgency and can be translated into, "Stop what you are doing immediately and freeze right now!" It's an opportunity to recalibrate.

If I could learn to stop, pause and check in with myself before answering a question or overreacting when my kids have a farting contest, I might find that the answers in my heart and soul are a lot different from the answers that come instantaneously blurting out of my big, fat mouth.

During the late 1890's Russian psychologist Ivan Pavlov studied behaviors in dogs and introduced all budding psychology students to the theory of classical conditioning and the concept of the repeated introduction of the stimulus, the bell and then a treat. He soon noticed the conditioned response of a wet, salivating dog. Anticipation itself caused the salivation. When Pavlov rang the infamous bell, the dog would salivate, knowing that the food was on its way. Pavlov even named this anticipation "psychic secretion."

In graduate school we were still studying how

stimulus and response operate in us humans, often without any awareness on our part. Stimuli are changes that occur around us in the environment. Most of us anticipate a shot in the doctor's office by cringing a little bit. When a mosquito lands on our arm, there is an automatic reaction that causes us to squish it as fast as we can. Both are everyday examples of stimulus and response.

I love Pavlov. He was a quirky dog lover who gave them lots of treats and gave us lots of fun ideas to work with in psychology class, but it was Viktor Frankl (1905 – 1997) who took the stimulus and the response to a deeper level. Frankl didn't focus so much on the stimulus or the response. He was more interested in "the space" or the time that exists between the stimulus and the response. For me, that space is the most valuable real estate in our brain. It is where our power lies, our power to choose how we are going to respond, and our power to be intentional. That is where you will find your truth. That is where you can pause long enough to hear your own voice.

That "space" is a place of wisdom. Sometimes you may only need a little bit of space. For example, if someone says, "Do you want a piece of red velvet cake?" It might only take you a second or two to know if you want the cake, but it is in that space before you answer that your will power has a chance to kick in. Bigger life decisions may require a lot of space. For example, if your employer asks, "Do you want to move to a new city for a big promotion?" Questions like that may require days or weeks of space before you are ready to make a decision.

The hardest questions are sometimes the ones in the middle. "Will you be the treasurer of our community bandstand?" Or, "Can I come and visit you for a week?" Or even, "Do you want to go out to dinner next weekend?" Our automatic response is often, "Sure! Sounds great!" But how many times have we said yes, and then later realized that we should have said, "Hell, no, I don't want to do that!"

That's why you have to remind yourself to OWN YOUR SPACE! It only takes two seconds to say yes, but often what you say yes to can take hours and hours, and maybe even years, away from your life. My mantra now is to always take at least one deep breath before saying yes to anything. I've also learned that the very best answer is, "Can I get back to you about that?" That creates even more "space" between the stimulus and the response. I think Pavlov would love me for that.

be still

Me and Don

There have been dozens of times I didn't hit the pause button and got myself into some crazy situations, but none were as impulsive as my post-high school getaway. It's a little embarrassing, and I'm kind of surprised that I am even admitting it to all of you. And it is definitely near the top of the long list of the dumbest things I have ever done.

Oops! I definitely forgot to hit the pause button.

Just out of high school I was the recipient of an unexpected, life-changing gift. It came in the form of a bullet hole in my right calf. It was an accident, but it left a big hole that could have easily ended my life.

Seconds before the bullet came through the garage ceiling and into my leg, I was dancing around my bedroom, happily packing and planning on leaving with some friends for a trip to Mexico that same night. Needless to say, the stray bullet ruined my plans, and I spent the night in the emergency room and the next several weeks on crutches.

The bullet hole got me thinking. After all, I could have died or been paralyzed. I was young and a free spirit and I didn't want to miss an opportunity to live fully, enjoy myself, travel and see the world. Who knows what other tragedies life might bring, right?

54

Two months later, I hugged my parents goodbye and boarded a flight to London alone. It was an adventure I will never forget. My eight-week vacation turned into over a year of freedom and serendipity, travelling through Europe without a care in the world. I slept on trains when I didn't have a place to stay, and when I did have a place to sleep, it was often in a smelly, deserted barn or on a pew in a small country church.

I never wanted it to end. But all good things must come to an end, or so I thought. One smoggy, dark day I landed at Los Angeles International Airport, where I was connecting through to San Francisco. Within hours I would be home and my worried parents would be so relieved and happy to finally see me again.

That was a different era in air travel. Tickets were cheap and transferable and somehow, well I do know how, because I was eavesdropping on a conversation at the phone booth next to me, I heard a few important words like "can't go, cheap, selling it." Turns out this kid had a ticket to sell to Honolulu for a ridiculously low price of $39.00 on some now defunct airline and he wanted to know if I wanted it. Well, hello. Of course I did.

Several hours later I called my parents from Honolulu. They thought they were never going to see me again AND that I had lost my mind.

While I was traveling around the island, I met a good-looking blond guy from Nova Scotia or Slovakia or somewhere cold. Anyway, he looked like he could be a fashion model and his name rhymes with Don Mannequin, so I'll just call him Don Mannequin because I don't know if his wife knows this story. So, Don Mannequin and I hit it off. No big romance or anything, but we were having a ton of fun exploring Honolulu together.

A couple of months later, my parents were again relieved to hear I was finally coming home, but not so happy that I was bringing Don Mannequin home with me. I assured them that we were just super good friends and that he would sleep in a different room.

Adjusting to being back at home was not easy, and I realized that soon I would need to get a job, go to college and settle down. Or, I could show Don Mannequin a bit of America and leave on a road trip with my old car and what was left of our money. We opted for one last adventure, filled the tank with gas, and off we went.

Don loved the Grand Canyon and camping in state parks, and I loved sleeping outside and looking up at the beautiful stars without a care in the world. Those were the days. We were winding down our trip, heading through Lake Tahoe with only about $130.00 left between the two of us. We figured we would have to get back to San Francisco by the next day.

That was, until we saw the sign. "Honeymoon Special." It was a small, quaint hotel. We had been camping for a long time and a shower sounded like a dream. And it was a complete package deal. For only $99.00 we could stay there for 2 nights, have all food included and all we had to do was get married! What a deal! And they would throw in a bottle of champagne to celebrate!

The ceremony went without a hitch, no pun intended, and Mr. and Mrs. Mannequin laughed and celebrated for two days straight. Reality did settle in once we returned home, but we went our separate ways, him to Nova Scotia or Slovakia and me to college and work.

Eight years later, Don Mannequin tracked me down and told me he wanted to get married, to someone else! Apparently he had looked into the legal status and discovered that we were still and quite literally Mr. and Mrs. Don Mannequin. He nervously wanted to know if I was willing to sign the divorce papers. Apparently, as I found out during dinner with him later that night, he had been quite successful in business and was a little frightened that I might want some kind of alimony. I'm sure he was delighted to fly in to have the papers signed because he walked into my lovely, bustling restaurant, only to realize that I was doing just fine for myself, too.

What was I thinking to have become Mrs. Mannequin? For a hot shower and a cold bottle of champagne. Could that really have happened? Oh, Mr. Mannequin, if only we knew about Pavlov and Viktor Frankl and the stimulus and the response… and the very important pause button.

A Man of Great Intention

Jimmy Gentry, an American hero who helped release the holocaust prisoners from the Dachau encampment, told me that he wanted to be intentional and kind every day of his life. He said he achieved this by adhering to the daily meaningful lessons he learned from his mother when he was a young boy. He believed in the traditions that were passed down to him and made a conscious effort to pass these values on to his own grandchildren and to anyone who would listen.

Mr. Gentry had a lifetime of heart-wrenching and beautiful stories, but he liked to tell the story of the last biscuit, which our family always loved to hear. It came from his mother and he said he really never understood it when he was younger. She raised nine children, and her husband died when the children were young. Money was scarce, and they often struggled to have enough food to eat, but she never allowed any of the children to eat the last biscuit on the platter.

Jimmy tells this story. "One day I really wanted the last biscuit, but she wouldn't let me have it. And when she picked up the plate with the last biscuit on it, I wondered what she was going to do with it. Then there was a knock on the back door. We lived near a railroad track and when she opened the door, there stood a hobo. He got the last biscuit. What she taught us is there is always someone who needs it more than you."

Over the years, Mr. Gentry has thoughtfully added passions and interests to his life. When I last visited him, he was 81 years old. We went to his painting studio, a small building on his farm, and he showed me his work. Even his artwork spoke of his intentional lifestyle. From his memory, he created art from his childhood and from his time serving our country. Each piece was a passionate slice of his personal history, as well as the history of America.

Mr. Gentry lit up when he talked about this

newfound passion and told me, "I just paint out of my head. And I didn't start painting until about four or five years ago when someone said, 'Why don't you paint?' I don't care whether I sell any of them or not. I just paint."

At 81, Mr. Gentry still enjoyed meeting new people and opening his family farm up every year for thousands of kids to celebrate the fall with hayrides, a cornfield maze and a pumpkin patch. He told me that he had a curiosity about people, and that one of his favorite things to do was to sit on a bench in downtown Franklin, Tennessee, and hope that someone would come by and ask him for help.

He stood by his values, lived intentionally every day, and never took the last biscuit.

be still

What I Love About Cancer

From my cancer journal:

A bald head, sunken eyes, and a flat chest are the evidence, clear as day. I know what you are thinking, no matter who you are. The outside appearance beckons friends and strangers to wonder if I am going to die. I get it. And I see it, too.

But what you all don't see are the more pertinent and mobilizing impacts of this disease that are taking place on the inside, the percolating undeniable wonder… not if I will die, but if I will live. What I love about cancer is that it has given me the opportunity and the awareness to fully and completely be alive. Maybe everyone already knows how to do that and I am just extremely slow, but, for me there were several keys to the castle that had remained hidden and out of my reach for many, many years. I only had a few certain keys, and I had just been opening the same old, creaky doors over and over again.

The keys I am finding now are the ones that give me the freedom in everyday life to put myself back near the top of that same gigantic totem pole that I fell off of many years ago. I suppose I am healing on the outside AND on the inside.

A lot of it comes from simply slowing down. I don't know that I would have ever slowed down if I hadn't been forced to. Would any of us? Here's a simple example. All my life I have felt the same way about stop signs…red means stop, green means go and yellow means accelerate, get through the intersection as fast as I can and then look quickly into the rear view mirror to make sure there isn't a cop behind me. But now I am slowing down a bit. Not in the old lady sort of way, but in a way that helps remind me

61

that the moments matter. So now I make it a point to stop at all yellow lights. I use that time to sing, be silent, pray or look around and pick out the most beautiful thing I can find wherever I am.

God created man in his own image. He told us, "Be fruitful and multiply; fill the earth and master it. Take charge of the fish of the sea, the birds in the sky, and everything crawling on the ground." Then he said, "I now give to you all the plants on the earth that yield seeds and all the trees whose fruit produces its seeds within it. These will be your food." God saw everything he had made, and declared that it was supremely good. God did not say it was supremely perfect!

We are not here to be perfect.

Lots of times in our house someone will say, "What do you think I should do?" And often the answer is our simple motto, "I think you should show up, and finish well." Sometimes the hardest part is showing up. So we remind ourselves that this is the essence of who we are, living in community. Showing up is part of what we are called to do as humans sharing this planet. We need to show up. But once we show up, then what?

Then we need to finish well. Everyone in our house understands that this does not imply perfection. Finishing well does not mean getting straight A's, winning the game, earning a perfect score, getting the job you wanted, or even the outcome you wanted. Finishing well means you can walk away knowing that you tried your best and did your best, with your whole heart. It's not about being perfect. Not at all.

Right Now

Dear Self,

You were created for this very moment. Right now is a fresh start, a do-over. Take the good lessons and the learning experiences from your life and carry them with you, for these are your stepping stones that have led you to today. Take the concrete burdens of shame, guilt and self-judgment that you are dragging behind you with every step and cut the ropes of bondage from whatever baggage you have collected. It does not serve you any more. Let it go. It's time to live your dream and find God's purpose for your life.

Your dream was inside of you before you were even born. It's your job to be still and listen to the song of your heart. You are extraordinary, beautiful, unique, and you were created for a special purpose. What do you think you were born to do? Like the famous words from Desiderata say so beautifully, "You are a child of the universe. No less than the trees and the stars, you have a right to be here!"

That means you are a child of the sun, and the moon, the planets and the stars. You are a child of the galaxies and all the cosmos. You are a child of God. You are significant and magnificent. So set yourself free. You are walking on the outside of a freaking planet, for goodness sake! How insane is that! Carry on in light and in lightness. Be intentional. And follow your JOY.

CHAPTER 5

Showing Up with Faith and Spirituality

"Stand tall. Lift your shoulders back and hold
    your head high," said the wind.

Her feet stand firmly planted in the earth. She is
strong.

Thoughtfully...
    With a contemplative rhythm,
        she reaches fearlessly
towards the light...

Time passes. She grows tall and glorious.

This is her journey…her belief…her faith…
    her knowing, trusting reply to the great unknown.

She understands.
If our Creator had wanted us to know…
        a cavern of our mind would be filled with
        that which remains a mystery.

She remains strong, yet flexible,
        like a field of ancient bamboo reeds,
        blowing in the breeze.

Willing to let the sunlight be her guide.

Her mighty branches stretch
        towards the arms of God.
But her roots tell the story.
Effortlessly she leans, and bows.
Yet she never forgets that she is a tree.

~ Diane R. Button

Research About Faith and Spirituality

Faith and spirituality are common themes in discussions of living life with a sense of purpose, but the word "spirituality" proves to have a wide variety of definitions and applications. From what my research suggests, spirituality is simply each individual person's private pursuit of, or relationship with, a Higher Power or God.

It is not necessarily religion, although it may be. On a collective level, it seems to be more of a relationship with and awareness of something bigger than oneself. From the interviews I conducted and conversations with hospice patients, an obvious contrast between religion and spirituality is evident. It is also clearly possible to be religious, yet not spiritual, or spiritual, yet not religious. One can also be neither, or both.

A Gallup poll in 2011 found that at least nine out of every ten Americans believe in God. In addition, according to past polls, 65% belong to a church, and 60% regard religion as an important component of their lives. A majority of people in America believe that many of the problems in the world today are based on divisiveness caused by religious practices and beliefs. These statistics suggest that spirituality, whether it is via formal religion or a private and personal definition, play an important role in giving people a sense of purpose and deeper meaning in their lives. This does not, however, suggest that a person who is an atheist or agnostic would not also feel their lives are meaningful or significant based on a different belief system, or even a lack of one.

Spirituality is personal, deeply internal, and a core foundation for a meaningful life. It is also almost impossible to define in a way that will fit all perspectives. It is derived from spirit, something unseen. Spirituality informs how we look at the origin of man, our purpose for being alive, and what we believe about what happens after we die. It is not religion, for it does not require formal structure. Spirituality does not label me right, or you wrong. It is not a belief, but a way that we are inspired to know God, or a concept of the divine that is greater than ourselves. It is a mindful awareness of how you belong, how you interact with the planet, what makes you want to get up in the morning, and how you show up for life.

My interviews have allowed me to understand the importance of knowing what brings people the closest and most intimate connection to God. Whatever it is, do that. Whether it be church, yoga class, tending the garden, taking a morning hike, playing the flute or dancing, do it with all of your heart and soul. Actually, any true and deep "feeling" in life offers up an opportunity to draw close to God. Grief and sadness do that, too, if you allow yourself to feel those feelings as well as the good ones.

Because spirituality is your own private pursuit of God, it does not need to be screamed from the mountaintops to be heard. And you don't have to search for it in the far corners of the earth because it is not hidden. The entire kingdom of God is the sweet, silence of the soul within you. It's already there.

Stories About Faith and Spirituality

Confessions

I have always respected the foundations of the Catholic Church, but as a child, I was a bit of a rebel. I'm not really sure why my parents sent me to a Catholic school. I rarely remember going to church on Sunday with my family, except for holy days or when I got to play my guitar in church and my parents wanted to watch. Sometimes I would ask my mom to take me when there was a cute boy who I wanted to see there and I needed a ride. Sometimes I would go with my friends and, although it wasn't cool to like church back then, I did.

There were only a couple of times that my mom made me go when I didn't want to be there. Usually that was when there was a cute boy who, for some reason, I didn't want to see that weekend. One time we pulled into the parking lot just as my favorite song came on the radio. I begged my mom to let us listen to it before mass, but failed to mention that it was the longest song ever recorded. I remember being so content, like I had won a big victory, sitting in the front seat of our old rambler station wagon, missing 8 minutes and 32 seconds of church and singing Don MacLean's huge hit "American Pie" at the top of my lungs.

At school we had to go to confession. I vaguely remember there was a certain time of year when we had to go every single day. It may have been Lent, and it may not have been every day, but it sure felt like it. We would stand in a single file line and one-by-one we stepped into the dark, wooden box where we privately told the priest our darkest thoughts and actions. After we received our penance for those atrocities, we made our way to the pew where we were to serve out our sentence, usually consisting of a holy cocktail of Hail Mary's and Our Father's and a couple other ones I can't remember. Sometimes we had to apologize to someone we had hurt, but that was usually for later at home.

Right before confession we had recess. After we finished our confession and subsequent prayers, we were allowed to return to the playground until the really bad sinners finished their prayers.

It didn't take long to figure out the system, even as 6th graders. To be able to continue to enjoy recess after confession, if you were in the middle of a heated 4-square game, then you would just say to the priest, "I was mean to my brother and sister." That way you'd just get one or two prayers and you'd be outta there and back in the game as soon as possible. You could also say you had mean thoughts or you didn't clean your room and you could be in and out in no time.

We used to talk about it while we waited in line.

"What are you going to tell Father?"

"I'm going to tell him that I was mean to my sister."

"That's what I was going to say. You can't steal my sin. Use something else!"

If you want to get out of confession quickly, never ever say that you hit someone, or that you lied to your parents, or stole candy from the local store. Any of those misdemeanors were punishable by a multitude of prayers and a longer time in the wooden box talking to the priest. There was no way you could ever finish a game of 4-square if you had lied or stolen something. So we saved the lies, the hitting and the stealing for days when we had more time to pray. We needed to throw the priest a good offense every now and then, just so he wouldn't catch on or think we were perfect.

be still

From Jack's Journal - Age 6

Kids make it seem so easy to connect with God. Jack was saying his prayers last night before bed. "Lord, please fill me with wisdom and lots of love. Keep filling me up with lots of wisdom and lots of love for my whole life and teach me to pray real good so that when I get to be a grandpa, I can be really good at praying for my grandkids. And Lord, I'll pray for them all the time and when I'm done praying, I'll come to see you and we can hang out and have a real good time. Does that sound fun?"

I Don't Know

All of my girlfriends seem to have a hard time asking for help. We all think we can do everything on our own. That's why things like flat tires, broken legs and cancer are so awesome for our growth. We realize that we really do need help and it's actually empowering to reach out and say, "I need help!"

Sometimes I also have a hard time saying, "I don't know." And sometimes I say really stupid things to mask the fact that I don't know. One time, on a particularly stormy night, I asked Jack to close his bedroom window. There was thunder in the distance and the forecast was for inclement weather throughout the night. Jack was enjoying the cool breeze, doing his homework and perfectly comfortable. There was no rain coming into his room and he was determined to understand why I wanted him to close his window. The truth is, I don't know why. But what I said was that I was afraid that lightening would strike and he might get hurt. That was literally the first stupid thing I thought and it came blurting out of my mouth.

Jack has not even remotely let me live that down. For years now, every time I ask him to do something that he doesn't fully understand he says, "Why? Are you afraid that lightening is going to strike?"

A few years ago Hannah, my curious and deep-thinking teen, was on a quest to know why she was born. At first I wanted to tell her all the stuff that sounds fluffy and that life will all make sense as she gets older. And then I wanted assure her that God has a plan and a purpose for her life, which I truly believe, even though that popular bible verse also doesn't answer the question. It's more like a comfort because of how complicated and inexplicable life really is. So I told her the truth. I don't know. And then she wanted to know if I thought she was born for a particular reason like to make the world a better place. I told her that I think so, and that she has already made the world a better place, and that I wonder about these things, too, but I really don't know. And then she asked what happens after we die? I told her that I have faith that it is beautiful and God will be there to greet her with open arms. That is my faith and that is what I want to believe, but I don't know.

If God wanted us to know the answers to these age-old questions of the world then there would have been an instruction guide attached to the umbilical cord. I didn't see one, did you?

I Can See Your Soul

I consider myself a Christian. Not a by the book, 110% all-in, card-toting obvious type of a Christian. I'm a bit of a closet Christian. I definitely cherry pick my favorite parts from the bible and I'm not the type who thinks anyone is going to hell. Period. The idea that one human being, created in the image of God, can tell another human being, also created in the image of God, that they are going to hell for what they believe, or don't believe, is just way too much for me to handle. I also can't imagine that God would have ever challenged Abraham to sacrifice his own son. I like the way the story ends, but the fact that it even happened just doesn't settle well with me.

I heard a pastor once say that a "true Christian" follows and believes the bible word for word. So I guess maybe I am just a bad Christian. But I don't think we are all going to get lined up in a row in heaven, where all the best Christians get the biggest trophies. I'm just doing what feels right to me, and doing my best to love and accept all people is part of that. And I do believe in the stuff that matters, like the resurrection and the words and teachings of Jesus. I also believe in "washing others feet" as a deep and powerful metaphor for humility and service.

There are many Christian friends of mine who are probably praying for my salvation at this very moment as they read this. But here's the truth. Many more of my friends are saying, "Amen, sister!" To all of you who have trusted me and shared your uncertainties, your lingering spiritual question marks, and your guilt for "faking it" for so many years with me, just know that you do not have to speak Christian-ese to live like Jesus.

Before I explain how I see God in everyday life, I'm adding here I have learned a lot from the Buddha, the Beatles, my kids, my yoga instructor, my dog Lola, my friends' parents, my hospice patients, my bonsai tree, and other teachers and religions, too. Either way, we are all lumped together in this melting pot called Earth. Apparently there is a universe "beyond" us, but I really don't get that either. I think when we talk about outer space we are forgetting that we are also in outer space. We just don't know all about it because we aren't supposed to know. So we get what we get in terms of spiritual teaching and religion, often starting with what our own parents tell us is true, and that leads us to what we believe and where we hang our faith hat. While uncertainty makes me anxious in everyday life, my faith hat is peacefully and calmly resting on the fact that there are mysteries of life that are intended to remain just that. Mysteries. The Great Unknown.

For me, spirituality starts in the heart. The heart is so much more than a blood-pumping organ. It is an emotional vessel, the foundation of love, faith, intuition, gratitude, grief and more. The heart is our symbol for love. We say "My heart goes out to you" and, "I will keep you close to my heart" and, "I love you with all my heart."

Clearly, the heart is correlated with love and, because of this, it also houses our pain and grief. My great-grandfather died when his children were only two and four years old. My great-grandparents were young and deeply in love when he fell ill with a rare and complex medical condition. After exhausting all medical treatment available in 1911, they boarded a ship and travelled across the ocean to the healing springs of Baden Baden, Germany, hoping for a cure.

Unfortunately, my great-grandfather died while they were in Baden Baden, and my distraught great-grandmother had to travel with my great grandfathers body back over the ocean to America. My great-grandmother tried to go on and raise her two young sons, but she could not function from the emotional pain in her heart. When she died her death certificate said she died of a broken heart. I have always believed this to be a possibility.

My grandfather, Charles Steiss, and his little brother Jack (1915)

This may sound kind of woo-woo or weird, but I believe the heart is the residence of our soul. The soul existed long before we were born, and I believe that the Creator of the universe embedded a soul inside the hearts of each and every one of us when we were born, and that is the part of us that is the image of God. Our soul. The fingerprint of God in each of us.

Mother Teresa said that every time she touched the hand of a leper or touched a body that reeks with a foul stench, she found courage and strength in her belief that she was touching God. She lived and breathed every moment with an understanding of our inter-connectedness as human beings. She saw the link to the divine in all souls.

So the heart is love. And God is love. And our soul is the Holy Spirit living inside of us. And we all have a soul, so we are all a slice of the divine. How cool is that?

When the meditating people say "Namaste" they are saying that the divine in me recognizes and honors the divine in you. In other words, they are saying, "I can see your soul." And when Mother Teresa says that she sees God in all beings, I think she is saying, "I can see your soul." We are all connected at the soul level. And when we die, our souls leave and only our lifeless empty bodies remain. In Hospice, we hear many stories of people having near-death experiences, where their soul is lifted up and out of their bodies, often towards a glowing light that feels safe and welcoming and peaceful.

When my mom had a life-threatening tumor in her pancreas, she had a radical operation called a Whipple. The pain was intense and I know at times she just wanted to die. One night, as I was sleeping upright in a chair by her bedside in the hospital, I awoke to my mom gasping for air. I noticed her oxygen mask was off and I yelled for a nurse. I grabbed the mask and turned up the oxygen as high as I could. The nurses ran in and did their magic on her until she began breathing again. They told me later that she came very close to death that night.

The next morning my mom woke up and immediately started telling me about her dream. "Oh, Dee," she said, "Last night I had the most beautiful dream I have ever had. I was lifted out of my bed and into a parade. It was colorful and joyous and so alive. Everyone was smiling and having a wonderful celebration." She went on to tell me that her parents were there, her aunt and her cousin, Gary were there, too. Everyone she had ever loved who died was there. She went on and on about the beauty and then she said, "It was so warm. The bright beautiful light filled every corner and all I could feel was love. Everywhere. Pure love. And it wasn't the everyday love that we all talk about. It was different and so unconditional and beautiful that it made me cry. I have never felt anything like that kind of love in my entire life. After last night, I will never be afraid to die."

Wow.

Amen.

Hospice patients teach me a lot about all the 7 components of a meaningful life, but none is more profound than the component of faith and spirituality. If you have not found peace with your spirituality before you are preparing to die, then it is often the time when life's biggest questions rise to the surface. The eyes of a dying person are deeper than anything you will ever see. They are filled with truth. And they are present and alive and so clear that it's almost as if you can see into the bottom of the ocean or even into eternity.

I believe that I am seeing their souls. I see the part that existed before they were ever born, that part that exists today, and that which will live on after they die. And that is our link, our common thread and our tapestry of humanity that weaves a web of love and compassion through us all. Imagine if every human had a musical instrument, all types of instruments but united in rhythm. Simultaneously we all play our G chord and, for that moment, there is perfect harmony. That is the music of our soul.

The Atheist

From my hospice journal:

A fellow human being suffering from physical pain is hard to watch. There are also emotional pains, like depression and schizophrenia, which can be debilitating and heartbreaking. Grief is hard, too. But I have never seen anything that looked more painful than the spiritual pain I witnessed today.

She's that story so many of us tell about the kid who was raised in the Catholic church, went to Catholic school and then ran as fast as possible to get away from the church and begin a life of rebellion against organized religion. Some return to the church. Others find a new path. But she was a self-proclaimed atheist. Yet her sister told us that deep down she missed the Catholic Church and her relationship with God, and she felt guilty, too.

The chaplain and I entered her bedroom and you could see the distress on her face. She looked like she was trapped in her body and couldn't get out. She was dying. She was crying. She kept sitting up and even stood and paced around her bed a couple of times. She hung on to her sister and then climbed back to bed. She was never still. She was afraid. There was a sad agony of restlessness in her spirit that was undeniable. She was not at peace.

We got to rub her legs and hold her hand. Our chaplain and I got to pray over her, and that made her relaxed and calm. She fell asleep, and she looked peaceful when we left. I may never know, but I felt that she was calling out for spiritual healing and a connection with our Creator before she could allow herself to die. Maybe she was trying to tell us that her bones were hurting. Maybe she was just angry. Maybe she was a fighter until the end. But I don't think so.

Spiritual suffering is painful, too. Not everyone has the same sense of who God is. We do not all worship the same God or believe the same story about what happens after we die. But when that day comes and you are lying on your deathbed, I encourage you to find comfort in knowing God, or at least to be at peace with your spirituality, whatever that means for you, so you can transition from this earth and feel that sense of peace that passes all understanding.

Auto correct can definitely be annoying, but who hasn't laughed until they cried at some hilarious typo. One time I meant to tell my kids that Gary would be there soon to pick them up from school, but instead the message said, "Farts will be here soon." Another time I reminded my son to "Bring your #2 penis for your Scantron test." My texting seems to change to "God" all the time. Like "Way better God on Hawaiian Airlines." Or "God to go." My favorite was on Easter when a devout Christian guy wrote a big group text to let everyone know that we should rejoice because "Chris is risen!"

Words are powerful tools. Back in the 90's I thought about starting a company, selling t-shirts and hats and buttons and such. They would all simply say, "Use me." It's provocative and edgy, yet deeply profound.

When I step into the home of a hospice patient, I try my best to leave my ego at the door. This is their time, not mine. I have come to serve. But it isn't always easy, so I know I can't go in there alone. So before I enter the house I pray, "Use me, God." Or sometimes I would recall the words of St. Francis, "Make me an instrument of thy peace." I know that it is not me who is the peaceful warrior rubbing the feet of a dying fellow human being. It is the power of God through me that gives me strength, courage and the words, or the silence.

Use Me

In the darkness of my empty heart
When life tries hard to tear me apart
I shout through the forest though I can't even see
And I cry to you through the deep, dark night...
Use me...

Stepping out into the joyous light
And for this season life seems all right
Still I sing with praise and give my life to you
Make my image yours and your glory shine through
Use me...

I know you've ordered all my steps,
You know my path and delight in my way,
But still I cry to you, Oh Lord
Please listen as I pray...
Use me...

I guess it's all part of my futile attempt to live like Jesus. One day I decided to follow the WWJD creed for an entire day. Before every word that came out of my mouth I thought, "What would Jesus say?" Before every bite of food I thought, "What would Jesus eat?" Before I went swimming, I wondered, "What would Jesus wear to the beach?"

At the end of the day, I was exhausted. It is so much easier just to blurt out whatever comes to mind, eat bacon from time to time and a little bit of dark chocolate, throw on some ratty worn old t-shirt and ripped shorts and throw the Frisbee on the beach with the kids. I just can't see Jesus doing any of that.

Still, I want to understand God and Jesus and how I can be less like a sinner and more like a saint. I believe that God sent Jesus to teach us how to love and have moral character and to give us the example of a "perfect" person. It's kind of weird though, because we will never be perfect like Jesus. If Jesus is a 10, then I am probably a 5 or a 6, some days a 4 and occasionally a 7, but very rarely. If I could just evolve up to a steady 8, that would be "perfect." Maybe Jesus isn't about being the perfect person, but more about understanding perfect love.

To me, Jesus is God's representative. What is so cool about Jesus coming here to visit us is that he spoke. Like, literally spoke, unlike God who either speaks in silence or in quiet whispers. That's why Jesus makes sense to me and I like him so much.

If I were more like Jesus this would be my to do list:

Be more humble.

Forgive freely.

Be less attached to material possessions.

Listen to God's calling on my life.

Be selfless and show up for others.

Stay grateful.

Be genuine and authentic.

Walk through life without judging others.

Not get angry or mean-spirited.

Never take advantage of others.

Never tell someone what to do.

Admit when I am wrong and apologize.

Strive for constant self-growth.

And if I could do a few miracles, that would be fun, too.

Hope Lives

Hope lives

inside the third line

of my favorite poem.

It lives

in the gentle unfolding of a flower petal,

in the sea foam gathered along the shoreline and

in birds flying in unison through the afternoon sky.

Hope lives

in gut-wrenching tears, and uncontrollable laughter,
and

in the eyes of a child and the touch of a wrinkled
hand.

Hope lives

in the cold sterile hospital hallway,

and in kitchens and hotel rooms

and in all the colors of the vegetable aisle.

It lives

where generations are gathered together

singing anthems of tradition, unity and pride

and then in the deep loneliness of a restless night.

Hope lives

in the distant villages and the dusty cities

From Bangkok to Africa to Rome

and in the sprouted weed along

a cracked sidewalk in Santorini.

Hope lives

in friends and enemies and dentists

and lawyers and hippies and heroes and

it even lives

in squirrels, lizards, eagles, tigers

and killer whales and snowy white egrets.

Hope lives

at the altar and the mosque

and the ashram and the synagogue

and on the corner of 41st[th] and Main.

It lives

in light and darkness and thunderstorm

and on the highest mountaintops

and even in the depths of the sea.

Hope lives

in every inhale and every exhale

and every beat of your racing heart

and it lives

in your very last breath when you release the heavy
load

and make your way to the light of eternity.

And then…

for years to come and even

for as long as forever

Hope lives.

Many Paths, Many Prayers

The morning of my double mastectomy I was flooded with kindness and support. There were people sending me white light, praying for me, lighting candles for me, sending me reiki energy, thinking positive thoughts, saying wishes of peace and reciting mantras of courage. One friend pinned my family's photo next to her photo of Pope John Paul on her wall. Another prayed with her beads that were blessed by the Dalai Lama. Many sent me uplifting and hopeful scriptures from the Bible and I received quotes from Buddha, Wayne Dyer, Maya Angelou, Viktor Frankl (my inspiration), Rick Warren, Deepak Chopra, the Bhagavad Gita, the Upanishads, John Lennon, and Albert Einstein.

I got prayers, positive vibes and healing energy from people we knew in Iraq, Turkey, New Zealand, Australia, Great Britain, India, Uganda, South Africa, and all across the United States. I got healing rainbow visualizations, intuitive messages, brightly colored auras and tons of virtual hugs and kisses. I got statues and essential oils and homeopathic ointments. I got songs and poems and was put on prayer chains all around the country. Some were praying every morning at 9:00am for 6 months. Others lifted me up in meditation during yoga classes.

I gratefully and graciously received every single gesture from around the world. It did not matter to me what religion my friend was at all. What mattered was that I was lifted up. I was lifted up so high and with so much strength and conviction and energy that it was like all the religions and spiritual practices of the world came together for me that morning and said in harmony, "We love you, sister. Don't worry. Every little thing is gonna be all right."

No wonder I healed so quickly.

CHAPTER 6

Showing Up with Acceptance

Pure white.
        Youthful… Energetic.
Pure white.
Simple.
  Elegant… Bright…Innocent
Endless possibilities.

Yet I crave
  Just one drop
Of yellow.
Sunshine…Happiness…
  Adventure.

—

Time passes.
And now I crave
  Just one drop

Of blue.
Settling atop the backdrop of soft yellow…
  The blue drop.

Powerful. Intelligent.
Over time a soft, grassy green.
New. Fresh. Full of potential.

And then I crave red
  Against the backdrop of fresh possibilities
  sits love, passion, fire.

I crave orange.
I crave purple, turquoise
and even
        chocolate brown.

Now I crave pure white.
But it is Thursday.
And I joyfully embrace
  my colorful life.

                    ~ Diane R. Button

The Research About Acceptance

Nietzsche said, "He who has a why to
bear almost any how." A reason or pu
can give a person the strength they n
their life, and give them hope and a reason to carry
on. Psychologist Victor Frankl lived by Nietzsche's
words while he was a prisoner in a concentration
camp. He had a reason to live, and that gave him the
motivation to carry on through unimaginable
hardship. He saw men in despair slowly give up hope
and then die. Again, he used Nietzsche's words and
told his fellow prisoners, "That which does not kill
me, makes me stronger." He encouraged them
further by explaining that no man knows what the
future holds, and that there was always a chance that
an opportunity would open up that would set them
free. It required accepting the moment, while still
hoping for a different future.

My research has revealed the importance of
acceptance in three specific areas: acceptance of
circumstances, acceptance of others, and acceptance
of self. Accepting our imperfect selves seems to be
the greatest challenge. It includes our bodies, our
innermost thoughts and also our feelings, reactions
and emotions. We are complex beings with a
multitude of pieces to each of our individual puzzles.

One person I interviewed told me repeatedly that the
secret of life is to be kind. If you are kind then you
are coming from a place of love. He learned that he

needed to be kind to himself, too. And that includes self-acceptance, which is a form of compassion and understanding that gives us the space to be fully ourselves.

There are many stories and many paths leading to acceptance. The common thread in my interviews was that everyone had hardships to overcome and obstacles in their path, and each person, with their own unique story and circumstances, eventually came to the point of acceptance. For some it was immediate, for others it took many years.

Sometimes at first glance acceptance doesn't seem like the best the answer or solution. Sometimes change is a more powerful choice. However, if there is suffering or sadness over a situation that cannot be changed, then acceptance can be the key for creating peace and emotional calm. This is because acceptance is not ever weakness. Acceptance is not complacent. It is awareness, truth, power and the ability to see the situation for what it is. This understanding may lead you to act because acceptance does not mean that you are a doormat or that you are simply taking what life gives you without reacting. Acceptance means that you get it, and that you see a situation for what it is in the present moment. This awareness gives you the power to choose. Acceptance may lead you to rise up, change directions or become a warrior for something you believe in.

And as we age, there is more we need to accept and often less we can control. As Joseph Campbell said, "The privilege of a lifetime is being who you are." Or another way of saying it comes from the delightful heart of Dr. Seuss, "Be who you are and say what you feel because those who mind don't matter and those who matter don't mind."

Show Up and Finish Well

Stories About Acceptance

Cool Like Pharrell

As the years go on I am much more accepting of who I am, what I have and also what I don't have. I used to find myself in an endless, unachievable and exhausting game of quiet comparison. One friend had an amazing and fulfilling job, and I envied her, even though I owned a popular restaurant and had a ton of freedom and success myself. I was jealous of another friend simply because she had a ton of friends. They were not the deep kind of friendships that grow roots that withhold the winds of any storm, but definitely this friend had friends that were like fields of bright green grass on a summer's day. Her friends filled every minute of every day and kept her busy having fun with all kinds of different people. And I envied that, although the idea of her frenzied life gave me immediate indigestion. I was jealous of other friends too, the ones with the skinny jeans, the pearly white teeth, the cute boyfriend, or the cozy party house. And there was the interior designer, the athlete with the killer abs, the one who could sing and the one who had a faith in God and such a deep spirituality that she always seemed like she was floating on a cloud.

Yep, I've been living a life of silent jealousy towards these assorted women for a long time, but I have finally begun to accept myself. I am learning how I fit into the dance of life, with my people, my circumstances, my choices, my joys, my problems, my fears, and my unique and authentic story. Life is a combination of good and bad, highs and lows, and there is always light at the end of the tunnel. Yet we always seem to be a work in progress, which doesn't seem particularly healthy either. It's not easy, trying to find our way in this crazy, beautiful world, but finally, in a milestone leap of self-acceptance, I unleashed the jealousy monster inside me and set her free.

Or so I thought. Recently my family was watching *The Voice*. I'm not much into TV, but that show is cool and that night it caught my eye. I was stunned to see my jealousy monster popping back up in a radical way! You might think I was jealous of the beautiful voice of the beautiful girl with the beautiful legs, the one who everyone was drooling over as she danced around with her beautiful alluring moves. But no, that wasn't it.

You see, I've evolved. I accept that I am no longer the beautiful, young girl in the room. I am the mom, the counselor, the wife, the friend, and the one who serves casseroles or quinoa to people who are sick.

And I thought that now I would be wiser and outside my "self" enough that I wouldn't have to feel those feelings any more when something popped up that triggered my jealousy. I felt satisfied in my soul that I matter too, that I am beautiful too, in my own saggy, aging way, and that I am exactly who I am supposed to be in this life.

But I realized that I wasn't quite the evolved woman I thought I was because it only took a second to backslide into jealousy again. Big time. Yet it wasn't any beautiful woman this time, no this jealously was wholly and completely directed at a man, one of the coolest men on the planet. His name is Pharrell Williams. It's true. I'm ridiculously jealous of Pharrell Williams. I can't help myself. He's just badass cool. He seems so wise, thoughtful and kind. He brings out the best in every person and he still says what he wants and needs to say in an authentic way. He's got unreal clothes and necklaces, which I desperately want. He always looks like he just meditated before he speaks, and then out flows something profound AND poetic! How does he do that?

I accept that I am aging. But I would be a lot more graceful about it if only I could be as cool as Pharrell.

be still

"Midnight Ramblings"

From my cancer journal, where lots of lessons about acceptance were learned:

Everyone who knows me well knows that my severe insomnia is both a blessing and a curse. My inability to sleep is the very reason I accomplish most of what I do in life. I love burning the midnight oil, but lately I have wanted to sleep so that I can heal. The doctor gave me sleeping pills, but told me not to take them all the time. I started to love sleeping through the night, and waking up with the morning sun, but soon discovered that the sleeping pills also made me get up and devour massive amounts of snicker's bars and kettle chips in the middle of the night. It's like sleepwalking. The first two times I blamed the kids for the random wrappers I would find in the morning, but the third time the crunching sound of half-eaten potato chips in my sheets when I got out of bed made me realize that it was me all along. These past few nights I have been back to my "normal" sleepless self, waking up sometime after midnight, ready to start the day. It is at these wee hours of the morning when I realize just how intense this thing called cancer really is.

Tonight I woke up with an old song playing in my head. I think it was a Joni Mitchell song, but it goes something like…

"Don't it always seem to go

that you don't know what you got 'til it's gone.

They paved paradise

and put in a parking lot."

It's still hard to believe it, but I think that's what happened to my body. They paved paradise... they took this familiar curvy chest of mine ... and put in a parking lot. Crazy. Last month I was this healthy person (or so I thought) and now I am a cancer patient. And it dawned on me that this is still the very beginning of my treatment. We will go tomorrow and find out what toxic combination of medicine I will be taking and for how long. Every part of my body will be bombarded in an effort to kill this intense beast called cancer. Hopefully, this poisonous cocktail will save my life, as it has for so many women before me. For that I am deeply grateful. But this is truly an invasion and an attack on my otherwise perfectly healthy body.

This brings me to my point. It's about these bodies of ours. So often we use such negative words and think such negative thoughts about what we look like, our shapes, our thighs, our saggy parts, our wrinkles, our aging, the parts that are too big and the other parts that are too small. We forget to be thankful for our health and all the wonderful ways

103

our bodies serve us every day.

And so now I get to live that other part of the song that says… "You don't know what you got 'til it's gone." And, in retrospect, I guess my flaws really weren't so bad after all. I wish I had been more accepting of myself over the years. And now, with a bald head, flat chest, giant scars, middle-aged chemo acne and a poofy tummy, I finally see that I am beautiful.

So next time you look in the mirror…I mean really look in the mirror… I encourage you to appreciate and be thankful for who you are. The amazing miracle of your body is truly a gift from God, made exactly as it was meant to be. Every single one of my friend's is truly BEAUTIFUL!!!   If I can see it, you should, too! No more complaining… we've got some living to do!

"Aaaarghh! It's Happening!"

More from my cancer journal:

I woke Mark up this morning with a screech: "Aaaargh! It's happening!" It wasn't a scream, just a loud screech. A cross between frustration and a muffled cry of helplessness; it was a screech loud enough to overpower the drone of the neighbors leaf blower. Then, it made its way down the hall and through the double doors to where Mark was sleeping. My hair is falling out. I think that's worth a screech or two. And I think I'm about to get a giant lesson in acceptance.

My graduate thesis is called "The Components of a Meaningful Life." Little did I know when I embarked on this topic that my graduate school thesis would end up in a head-on collision with my life! I am nearly finished, so whenever I have the energy, that's what I do. My goal is to complete the written portion before my next chemo treatment next month. It's going to be close.

Through my thesis research, I have concluded that there are seven components to a meaningful life. Right now I am working on the component called acceptance. With the people I interviewed, all of whom are over 70, this means accepting themselves, accepting others and accepting the circumstances of their life. It's ironic to be writing about this topic on the very week that I am about to become bald.

I woke up this morning, got in the shower and my hair started falling out in chunky clusters, like if you pulled someone's hair when you were a kid, and it actually came out. Later when I brushed it, it was EVERYWHERE. I'm sure I lost about 20% this morning. The screech, though loud, still had an "acceptance" tone to it.

I'm sure I was in denial until today. I'm sure that deep down I thought I would be the one and only person to have their hair remain perfectly intact while on Adriamycin. Or maybe not. It looks like I need to find the wisdom those in my study seem to be talking about…ACCEPTANCE. This one isn't so easy… not when your femininity is falling out and running down the shower drain!

Twenty years and counting… Lucky me!

But writing now, I think about my husband. When I cried and told him how "unfeminine" I felt, with my balding head, no breasts, pimples from the chemo, scrawny body and bloated tummy, he just hugged me for the longest time. He told me that I was beautiful for so many reasons besides those, and that my beauty will last forever. He has accepted me completely and given me a place to rest my weary, fuzzy head. That is ACCEPTANCE. It made me grateful that we have taken the time to nurture our relationship over time, because when cancer came, we had each other.

A dear friend wrote me a card yesterday and it said "Life is not about waiting for the storm to pass; it's about learning how to dance in the rain!" There really is no better time than the present...to learn... to love... to grow and to simply dance. It took every grain of strength I had in my body to swing my hips and dance in the shower.

be still

A Hole So Big

From my hospice journal:

Today I started my first support group meeting as a grief counselor at Hospice. Friends have warned me to guard my heart and wondered if I, after just surviving breast cancer, should be volunteering for a position that requires surrounding myself with loss, death and grieving all day. They wonder how I will cope as others are dying of cancer, or how I will respond when a person shows up who just lost a young spouse, like Mark did just before I met him.

There is a peace right now and I cannot say for certain that it surpasses "all" understanding, but it is real and merciful and I know this is where I am supposed to be. An unknown author once said so beautifully that "being at peace does not mean to be in a place where there is no noise, trouble or hard work. It means to be in the midst of those things and still be calm in your heart." I get this. And I choose to be calm in my heart.

As fate would have it, only two people showed up for our meeting. One was a mom who had suddenly lost her young, newly married daughter to an undetected genetic medical condition. The other was her daughter's husband. His story is familiar to me. I recognized his pain, his hopelessness and his desire to go to bed at night and never wake up again. I saw that same look in Mark's eyes after his first wife, Ronnie, pregnant with triplets, died suddenly of a brain aneurysm. Mark was understandably a hurting, empty shell. So, in my meeting that night, I fully understood when the spouse looked at me with grieving eyes and asked, "How can someone so small leave a hole so big?"

Grief. It's a full body physical kind of thing. It comes in waves and often at unexpected times. It's individual. There is no timeline. There is no "correct" way to grieve. And anyone who tells you it will be better in a year, or after you celebrate the "first" holidays without the person you love, is really just hoping or guessing about how you will feel.

Grief. It is your body's natural response to loss. It manifests itself in strange places in your body. It hurts. It is often lonely. But, the body knows how to grieve. It knows how to breathe. It knows how to give birth and it knows how to die. The body knows how to grieve, but we must let it happen.

Grief. It's not an emotion that we can put in a box, or save to pull out one day when we are ready to deal with it. No, grief is not like that. We may be able to stop crying or put on a happy face for a while, but the grief is still there in that empty hole in our chest. We grieve about the past because of the memories we cherish or maybe we grieve over circumstances that were not pleasant. We grieve about today because we ache and we miss the person who has passed or the love that is lost. We grieve about tomorrow because we will not share that day with the one we loved. All of the things that were going to be are now gone and we must start anew. And we don't want to.

Grief. It's like anger, hate, pain or jealousy. It's an unwelcome emotion that we often try to hide from. But if we do not welcome it, then we are not feeling. If we are not feeling, we cannot heal. The reason we feel grief is because we allowed ourselves to first feel love. Perhaps the pain and sadness of loss will always be there, but someday, as the stages of grief circulate through our aching hearts, we may get to a place that feels like acceptance.

be still

The Mask

It seems like we all want more. We want more money. We want more sleep and more free time. We want more sex (well, some of us do). We want more food and more wine. We want more room in our houses and more technology to distract us. We want more, more, more. How will we ever stop to enjoy the beauty of what we have if we do not understand that we already have enough? We don't need more. We need less of just about everything except love and friendship. Abundance is awesome in our garden, but not in our closet!

We have enough. And we are enough.

My daughter, Carly, has learned this lesson the hard way. Once she said she had been "wearing a mask" all her life. More accurately, she had been wearing many masks, changing them as needed to fit the situation or the people she was with. Each mask was painted in multi-colored hues and sculpted into elaborate masterpieces. Though remarkably different, they provided the same purpose, which was to reach out and say, "Look at me. Like me. Can't you see that I'm you're type of person." Along the way, after changing masks so often, she forgot what her own type of person was. She morphed from one cocoon to another, never pausing long enough to love herself and to develop into the beautiful butterfly that she is.

Self-discovery, life experience, and the hands of time are now teaching her that she was wasting her own life by living a life designed for someone else. She had forgotten who she was born to be. There is freedom in knowing who you are, honoring that being and walking along the path of life that is paved uniquely for you…even if you have to walk alone sometimes.

Carly told me one day that she had made a conscious decision to shed her mask. It's gone and traded in for the truth. No more hiding. No more being the social chameleon. She is focusing on knowing herself and belonging rather than trying to fit in and be popular for shallow pleasures. Granted, there is still a bit of glue, tape and some sticky pieces left, but she is beginning to pick them away, bit by bit.

Stop and Smell the Sunflowers

From my window during chemo:

Sweet Hannah is planting seeds in tiny pots. Basil, oregano, sunflowers, marigolds, chives and more. Watching her enthusiasm, it occurred to me that I have reached a place where I can enjoy life on so many levels and some of the best moments are the most simple. It is a joy and a privilege to watch Hannah grow up. It has become fun to work on school projects, go on bike rides, braid her long, blond hair, or plant seeds, often right at the moment I should be cooking dinner.

Sunflowers are my favorite flower. I love it that Hannah is planting a small seed for me, in hopes that it will one day be a tall and glorious masterpiece, the showcase of our back yard. But guess what? I have also learned that it may not be God's will for me to live to see that sunflower, but I can still enjoy the seed.

be still

Not Fair!

Some things in life are simply not fair.

We live on an amazing street filled with all different

types of people who look out for each other and care about our community. It's special because most of us don't have family close by, so we rely on each other to open our homes for holidays and social gatherings. Our plan is to all grow old together and sit on our porches, in our rocking chairs, talking story as we say in Hawaii. We hope to cook in shifts and eat together several times a week, making cooking more of a social event, rather than a chore or a necessity.

The other thing is, we are all generally the same age. Well, almost. One exception is the beautiful couple, who actually live in Austria, but they come and go and we all love them to death. Well, almost. I must admit, it's that beautiful people thing that kind of gets in the way. I want to hate them, but they are so damn friendly and fun that I just can't.

Hannes is a chiseled athlete who does extreme sports including competitive racing in air shows. He's on TV and I guess kind of well-known, so he likes to come over to our street where people don't care about that kind of stuff. Well, almost. The problem is really Miriam, his European model pencil-thin perfect body great teeth always happy wears little clothes all the time fun-loving girlfriend. She's just too beautiful. I can't imagine what it's like for guys to talk to her because I even actually find myself drooling a little bit when I'm around her.

One night we were at a party at Hannes and Miriam's house and everyone was having a wonderful evening. It was getting late and I was thinking it was time to go, but Miriam pulled out a couple of beautiful Austrian etched bottles and said, "But wait, before you go you must try this. It's from Austria."

My crazy friend, Twila, as usual, told me I should stay and try it, but I was skeptical.

The bottles were like exquisite pieces of art, and Miriam gently opened the top of one and let me smell what was inside. If I didn't know better, I would swear it was poison. It smelled flammable and dangerous, like something you may use to commit a crime. I thought to myself, there was no way I would ever drink a sip of that. "What is that?" I asked with a tone that probably let her know I wasn't too excited to try it but wanted to be nice.

Miriam smiled at me with her tall, skinny, healthy, glowing self and said, "It's a grappa. It is wonderful for your body, and your skin, and especially helpful for your digestion. I drink it every night after dinner…every single night." Then she rubbed her tummy and smiled even more. Was it possible that this was her fountain of youth?

Hmmm. At that point I began rethinking this. If it's that good for her then I'll try some, and you never know, maybe when I wake up in the morning I will have good digestion AND be six-feet tall and have the perfect body. Why not, it obviously works for her!

So I drank a hefty shot of the liquid poison from Austria and made my way home, anxious to get to bed so that I could wake up and see the results.

The next morning, I woke up 3 pounds heavier, with a raging headache and feeling like I was gonna barf. Not fair!!!

But in the end, I know, it's not about becoming a new person. Besides, if I were 6 feet tall, I would just have eight more inches of body parts to worry about. I'll just stay focused on belonging in my tribe and being the best person I was created to be. I refuse to have a bad relationship with my quirky, adorable, imperfect self.

CHAPTER 7

Showing Up with a Positive Attitude

Awake with open arms…
accepting all the glory that
another day shall bring.

Walk through the day…simply
unattached
and undeniably free.

The calm pace…
respite from the hamster wheel,
makes the heart slower to judge
and more open to compassion and
forgiveness.

Every moment is a choice.
   A response.

Night falls.

Let it all go….
   in hopes that tomorrow begins
   with another moment to

Awake with open arms…

                              ~ Diane R. Button

The Research About a Positive Attitude

A positive attitude starts with positive thinking. In the field of positive psychology, positive thinking helps people see the glass half full, or a light at the end of the tunnel. Rather than digging deep into dysfunction, mental illness and problems, the positive psychology model helps people to become happier and healthier people in all ways. Sometimes a person needs to dig deep to work through issues before they can get to this place, but many of us just need to change how we think.

What my interviews have shown is that most people are generally happy beings who thrive with healthy, loving social support systems and meaningful work. We want to be optimistic, positive, and live joyful, purposeful lives.

Viktor Frankl lived through one of the greatest tragedies the world has ever known, the Holocaust, and survived to share his experiences with the world. Though he contemplated the meaning of life even as a young boy, it was during that time of suffering that he became the most clear and really came to understand the meaning of life. In his book, *Man's Search for Meaning*, he describes life in the concentration camp. He lost everything of any external value, but Frankl has personally observed and experienced that life has meaning and purpose, even under the most extreme conditions. Frankl describes moments of contentment and peace while suffering through the most treacherous of circumstances. It was at these moments in the concentration camps when he realized that he still felt fulfilled. In addition to his memories, he had his dignity, his attitude and his inner values, which were anchored in his deep spirituality, and could not be taken away, even in the darkness of the camp environment. To choose his attitude was the last of his human freedoms.

An anonymous author illustrates the importance of a positive and healthy attitude in life: "Life is 10% what happens to you and 90% what you do with what happens to you." A person can look at the proverbial glass as half empty or half full. Attitude is a choice that each person makes every day and every moment. Humanistic psychologist Carl Rogers said, "The good life is a process, not a state of being. It is a direction, not a destination."

Some people I interviewed took many years to discover the impact of their attitude on their overall well-being. But when they understood the power of their thoughts, and the fact that they could choose their attitude, they became more content and peaceful. Indicators of a positive attitude include compassion and kindness, forgiveness, letting go of negative or self-defeating thoughts, being mindful, finding joy and peace in daily pleasures, being open-minded and tolerant, growing through hard times, and having realistic expectations.

In summary, if you want to change your life, start with changing your thoughts. Taking a "look on the bright side" has benefits that make life better. Think about who and what you love. Think about what you can do and what you want to do. Think about the beauty, the good and the joy in your life and the world around you. The positive thoughts and emotions will help you see the endless possibilities available to you in life. As Shakespeare said, "There is nothing good or bad, but thinking makes it so."

Show Up and Finish Well

Stories About a Positive Attitude

You Are a Masterpiece

One day, while on vacation in Mexico, our family went to visit an orphanage in San Miguel de Allende. The kids had saved some money and wanted to do something good with it. They were hoping to find some ways to serve the needy children and make their lives better. As is often the case in these situations, we thought they needed help and went there to give, but in the end, we were the ones who walked away with the golden nugget of wisdom.

The director of the orphanage, Victor, is both an artist and a builder. He has a reputation for taking the most decrepit and seemingly useless scraps of wood and materials he can find and turning them into functional, decorative pieces of furniture and other necessities that the home cannot afford to purchase. The boys in the home helped him build a beautiful addition on to the side of the house, an outdoor sitting area, with a rooftop made from old palettes that were going to be discarded.

While building these masterpieces, Victor explains to the boys how some people may think that these items are useless and not worth restoring or salvaging, and some people may just cast things aside or throw them away. But in truth, these items are valuable and can be used for great things. He tells them that this is the same for each of them. Some people may not have valued these kids or seen their potential, but Victor did. He sees them each as a unique, important, useful and creative being, filled with the potential for greatness. In his eyes, each one is already a masterpiece and his confidence in them shines through in ways that make them believe they are perfect in their imperfections and their circumstances, just like all of us.

You cannot fail with a mindset that sees each and every person as a beautiful masterpiece.

Mahatma Ghandi said that nobody could hurt you without your permission. Why give your power or your joy over to a grumpy or negative person? We always have a choice. As a matter of fact, all day we are making choices. Studies show that we make about 612 calculated and voluntary decisions each day. That's a lot of free will.

This short story by an unknown author illustrates how much power we have in regards to our personal choices and how we decide to respond to everyday situations that cross our path:

I walked with a friend to the newspaper stand the

other night, and he bought a paper, thanking the owner politely. The owner, however, did not even acknowledge him.

"A sullen fellow, isn't he?" I commented as we walked away.

"Oh, he's like that every night," shrugged my friend.

"Then why do you continue being so polite to him?" I asked.

And my friend replied, "Why should I let him determine how I am going to act?"

be still

"Cleared for Chemo"

From my cancer journal:

This was a beautiful week! Getting out and driving past the colorful trees filled my heart up and made me remember how big and magnificent this world really is. The fall colors in Tennessee remind me of driving south through the tunnel in Sausalito, California and popping out the other side with a glorious view of the Golden Gate Bridge, with the fog hanging heavy in the sky. They remind me of rainbows in Hawaii and driving through the pineapple fields, suddenly coming over the hill and looking at the ocean in the distance with the waves crashing along the shoreline. God is so much more and so much bigger than cancer or chemo or my safe, little bedroom.

My attitude has shifted. It was good before, but there was this underlying fear I couldn't shake. It was about chemo. When I found out the PET scan was clear, I immediately started talking myself out of doing chemo altogether. Who needs an extra 13% chance of living 10 more years? Ok, well maybe I do. But then I started bargaining with myself, and considering postponing chemo until January. But then, just as I was about to start feeling sorry for myself, something profound happened. I started looking forward to chemo!

It happened like this. I was on antibiotics that I took once a day for a wicked infection. There were 10 pills and the last pill was to be taken today, Sunday, the day before chemo. So that made me mad because I really can't stand taking drugs and I thought that I will just be on drugs from now until I finish the Tamoxifen in 5 years. So every time I opened the antibiotics I counted them, realized how many days were left before I start chemo, and thought to myself, "9 days until I get poisoned," then "8 days until I get poisoned." Great attitude, huh?

It occurred to me on day six, as I was opening the bottle, that I had a choice. Do I climb the mountain or do I crawl into the cave? I opened the bottle and I thought, "Thank you, God, for chemo. Chemo is NOT poison and it will NOT kill me. Chemo is medicine and it is designed to keep me alive. Chemo is part of the healing process. Thank you for my healthy body that will handle this treatment. Thank you for the wisdom in the medical field, for the technology, for the progress and for the hope that is chemo."

We don't always get to choose what happens to us in our lives, but we always get to choose what our attitude will be.

And now it is Sunday. And I choose to feel peaceful.

This may be the most frequent Internet story I have ever received. I don't know if everyone has heard it already, or if everyone just knows what to send me!

I Love It

Today, a 92-year-old, petite, well-poised and proud man moved into a nursing home. This man is fully dressed each morning by eight o'clock, with his hair fashionably coifed and shaved perfectly, even though he is nearly blind. His wife of 70 years recently passed away, making the move necessary. After many hours of waiting patiently in the lobby of the nursing home, he smiled sweetly when told his room was ready.

As he maneuvered his walker to the elevator, the nurse provided a visual description of his tiny room, including the eyelet sheets that had been hung on his window.

"I love it," he stated with the enthusiasm of an eight-year-old having just been presented with a new puppy.

"Mr. Jones, you haven't seen the room; just wait."

"That doesn't have anything to do with it," he replied. "Happiness is something you decide on ahead of time. Whether I like my room or not doesn't depend on how the furniture is arranged, it's how I arrange my mind. I already decided to love it. It's a decision I make every morning when I wake up."

That sweet man has the ultimate positive mental attitude. It keeps me strong and courageous and reminds me that I have a choice; I can spend the day in bed recounting the difficulty I have with the parts of my body that no longer work, or get out of bed and be thankful for the ones that do. Each day is a gift, and as long as my eyes open, I'll focus on the new day and all the happy memories I've stored away, just for this time in my life.

Thich Nhat Hanh said, "People usually consider walking on water or in thin air a miracle. But I think the real miracle is to walk on earth. Every day we are engaged in a miracle which we don't even recognize: a blue sky, white clouds, green leaves, the black, curious eyes of a child- our own two eyes. All is a miracle." And speaking of miracles, another way of looking at our attitude is through the eyes of Albert Einstein who said that there are two ways to live your life, one as though nothing is a miracle, and the other as though everything is a miracle. The choice is yours.

All the Happy People

Generally, I am a positive person and can find light in the darkest places. But lately I have become sick and tired of all the happy people posting on Facebook – that's why sometimes I call it Fakebook. I don't know, maybe I'm just jealous that everyone else is living such a glamorous, adventure-filled, cheery life, and I am always folding laundry, paying bills and checking for new signs of aging. My friends are always posting about their amazing kids, and the incredible perfect love they have for their husband, and the adventure of a lifetime they just returned from. I suppose I do it, too. Carly won this award, and Jack was in the newspaper again, and Hannah came in 7th in the world at the Extreme Cowboy Race in Texas. Hey everyone, take a look at our high-functioning, successful family! Yep, our badges of glory are all there, but for me it seems that the truth lies somewhere between our Facebook posts and something not quite so pretty.

But really? Are we all having that much fun?

If I were totally honest and posted the "real" stuff every day, no one would be my Facebook friend. I would depress everyone and I would sound like a whiner, which I am not. My FB page would say:

"Today I went grocery shopping."

"Today I cleaned the house."

"Big day! Today I cleaned the house AND went grocery shopping. "

"Today my teenagers treated me as if I have had a lobotomy and am actually the most stupid human on earth. I seriously don't understand why in the world so many people have children. Then I went grocery shopping."

"Today I asked Mark if we could talk about our summer plans and he just kind of grunted out this weird dinosaur sound that I think meant that he wasn't into talking about the summer. I hope you all enjoy your trips to Bali and Patagonia!"

You Don't Know My Story

I was having coffee with a friend of mine in Nashville when a woman came into the coffee shop in a puddle of tears. She was speaking loudly and sobbing uncontrollably to someone seated at the table next to us. My heart broke for her without even understanding why she was crying. Within minutes everyone in the coffee shop knew that her brother had just died suddenly and she was trying to get her kids organized so she could fly out to be with her parents. It was agreed that her friend would pick her kids up from school and she would get home, grab a few essentials and make her way to the airport.

I left the coffee shop and ended up behind the crying woman at the first stoplight. The light changed and she pulled out and inadvertently made a left turn a little bit too fast and wide. Within seconds, a car, obviously driven by an insecure man with a tiny umm...brain, pulled up along side of her and started honking, flipped her the bird and yelled, "Get off the road, you stupid bitch." My heart broke all over again. I just wanted to tell that guy, "Be kind. You don't know her story."

Someone told me a story once, I think it was originally told by author and spiritual teacher, Jack Kornfield, about a man who was impatiently waiting in a long line at a busy department store while the clerk was talking to the customer at the check-out counter. This clerk was even taking time to hold the customer's baby and carry on a conversation while the line continued to grow.

Of course, these are always the moments when we get to choose how we will react to the situation. Will we use the time to breathe and relax, and smile at the sweet loving interaction unfolding at the checkout counter? Or will we get irritated and maybe even make some snarky remark when we finally make our way to the checkout counter? Somehow that day, the person in line managed to quell his own frustration. When it was his turn to check out, the clerk thanked him for being so patient. And then he heard the story. This little baby belonged to the clerk, and her friend brought the adorable baby to the store once or twice a day for a hug from mom, who was sadly mourning the loss of her husband in the war.

You just never know what the person that God put in your path is going through. I always tell my kids, "Be kind. You don't know their story."

Happiness

A woman taught at a community college in Tennessee. She loved her job and the multitudes of personalities that came through her door seeking a better future. She loved that she was making a difference in the lives of some of the young adults, but noticed the spark was missing from so many of them, as if they were partially deflated balloons that were once flying high with helium and hope.

One day the woman's daughter, a kindergarten teacher, was feeling ill, so the woman went to fill in for her daughter. She stepped into a room filled with noise, energy, laughter, smiles and primary colors. The room was alive with happiness and joy.

She wanted to get to know the class so she introduced herself and then asked them, "How many of you can draw?" and every little hand in the room was instantly raised high up in the sky.

"How many of you can dance?" Again, all hands were eagerly raised.

"How many of you can solve a crossword puzzle?" Again, the hands went flying in the air.

The next day she returned to her own teaching job with the college students. She watched with a tinge of sadness as the glum, long faces came strolling in, one by one, a far cry from the energy of the kindergarten classroom she had experienced the previous day.

She opened her notes to begin her lesson, but stopped herself and looked into the tired, lifeless crowd and asked them, "How many of you can draw?" No one raised a hand.

"How many of you can dance?" No one raised a hand.

"How many of you can solve a crossword puzzle?" No one raised a hand.

What did the world present to these kids over the years that caused them to lose their sense of playfulness, curiosity, joy and personal ability? When did the word "can't" become an epidemic? Clearly, everyone can dance, but maybe they feel insecure or not good enough, or worry they will be laughed at. Oh, to learn to navigate and live on the planet with the same sense of sheer joy, and wonder, and freedom of expression as a kindergartener would indeed be a freeing experience.

Personally, I think it's partially because we all try too dang hard to be "happy." We need to remember that happiness is a fleeting emotion. It isn't sustainable or lasting. We are happy because we got a job, or met someone special, or because it's Friday. I was happy once because I found half of a bag of dried up red vines in the console of my car.

Life is a series of ebbs and flows and sometimes we get to ride the happy wave but inevitably that wave will come crashing down and we ride another wave until the next set comes in.

We always hear, "I just want to be happy." Or, "I don't care where my son goes to college, I just want him to be happy." Happiness is fun, but the true challenge in life is to find contentment. Contentment is lasting. It means that there is a sustaining and perfect peace, regardless of the circumstances. It comes from deep in our soul and it says, "I am here, all of me, showing up for whatever life brings my way. I will endure the hard times and rejoice in the hard shit and I will do it all with an open heart, knowing that I am significant and this is part of my journey in life." Bring it on. The peace in the chaos is contentment.

Buddha wandered for many years seeking the nature of our existence. He became aware that some thoughts lead to suffering and other thoughts lead to contentment. It's a choice. It's an attitude.

be still

A Good Hair Day

A woman woke up one morning, looked in the mirror, and noticed she had only three hairs on her head. "Well," she said, "I think I'll braid my hair today."

So she did and she had a wonderful day.

The next day she woke up, looked in the mirror and saw that she had only two hairs on her head. "Hmmm," she said, "I think I'll part my hair down the middle today."

So she did and she had a grand day.

The next day she woke up, looked in the mirror and noticed that she had only one hair on her head.

"Well," she said, "Today I'm going to wear my hair in a pony tail."

So she did, and she had a fun, fun day.

The next day she woke up, looked in the mirror and noticed that there wasn't a single hair on her head. "YAY!" she exclaimed. "I don't have to fix my hair today!"

Attitude is everything.

~ Author unknown

Hope Wins

It occurred to me tonight that often just about everything we have to be thankful for is right before our very eyes, especially on Thanksgiving Day. As you gather together with your friends and family, with all the hustle and bustle and laughter and noise, I encourage you to stop for just a moment, be silent, and simply look around the room.

Notice the walls that protect you, the heat that warms you, and the colorful holiday table that you are likely sitting at filled with an abundance of food and festive drinks. Look at everyone in the room and you will see someone who you love deeply, or someone who knows who you really are and understands your heart, or someone who encourages you when you are feeling down.

When silence fills the room, there is only one thing that remains, the most important part of who we are, the main ingredient of Thanksgiving, the greatest gift of all, and that is love. And to know love is so much more precious than all of our worldly possessions, and for that, I am thankful.

But this year, in my silent times, I've noticed a new feeling, a deep and stirring feeling in my heart. It's not about today. It's about tomorrow, a better tomorrow, for us, for our kids, and for what is truly important. It's not easy and many people are struggling. In some ways the world is bruised and battered. Hope wins, and love wins too, when we are blessed with the important things like friendships to cherish, hearts to feel and eyes to see, mountains to climb and hands to hold. Those are the real blessings that don't fluctuate with the economy or the stock market. No one can take these things from us. And when I stop to remember these special things, hope wins.

And even though our country is divided on so many levels, we have taken some giant steps forward. We, as a nation, have our freedom and a chance to come together and have all our voices heard on Election Day. While the news reports tell a bleak story of a spiraling infrastructure and an unsafe world, I see one person at a time making a difference, doing what they can, day by day. And for this, hope wins!

And when we look into our children's eyes, when we hear their voices, their laughter and their dreams, when we pour our hearts into them and begin to see a glimmer of the goodness that will be our future and theirs, then hope wins.

So next time you are gathered with your family and friends, I encourage you to look around the room. Take it all in. There is so much. There are the memories of yesterday, the love that is today and the hope that is tomorrow. And for all of this, I am grateful. And hope wins.

Show Up and Finish Well

CHAPTER 8

Showing Up with Love and Relationships

Sit with me,
>For if you are not near me
You will not know my story.

Listen to me,
>For if you do not hear my words
You will not know my story.

Cry with me,
>For if we have not shared the depths of my soul
Then please do not judge me

For truly,
    If you have never cried with me
Then you cannot know my story.

~ Diane R. Button

The Research About Love and Relationships

From attachment in infancy until our final days, the impact of love and relationships is one of the most rich and enduring components of each of our lives. The founding father of psychoanalysis, Sigmund Freud said, "Love and work are the cornerstones of our humanness. Love and work... work and love, that's all there is."

Our families, our legacies, and the strong link of the generational chain form the foundations of how we value, define and nurture our relationships. Child development specialist and author Laura Berk says that one of the main reasons most people in today's society still choose to have children is the innate desire to give and receive warmth and affection. This reasoning was consistent throughout my interviews, along with the idea that the indescribable bond for the first child was deeper than one could ever imagine, then the concern that one could not love the second child as much, and then the eventual understanding that there is plenty of that love to give and receive. Many people I interviewed said that raising their children is the aspect of their lives that is the greatest contribution they have made to the world, partially because they feel they parented well, it was rewarding, and their children were thriving.

Mother Teresa said, "Love does not measure, it just gives." This giving and loving without measuring is an important concept in building a meaningful life. Psychologist Erik Erikson believed that our final stage in life will be one marked with either fulfillment and what he called ego integrity, or one filled with regret and despair. Ego integrity vs. despair was the term Erikson chose for his final stage of psychosocial development. However, it takes a lifetime of seven other stages to get to this point. The choices one makes along the way, even with life's ups and downs, ultimately lead to a range of possible outcomes at the final stage of life. To have ego integrity would be to have fulfillment, contentment, balance and a sense of peace about how you fit into the world. The conscious effort to live a life that would ultimately lead to this place was the initial impetus for my thesis, although the wisdom and impact of Viktor Frankl assured me that the seven components that I had identified for a meaningful life were valid and accurate.

Due to the Hospice movement and improving the quality of end of life care, much has been written in recent years addressing the needs of the dying. This literature reveals many answers to what it is that people value at the end of their lives. This road leads to possibilities for discovering ways people can live their lives, when they are still young, with a goal towards authenticity and ego integrity, so that they will not face the despair of unfinished business in their final days. Despair and accompanying fear at the end of life almost always has to do with love and personal relationships, unspoken words, forgiveness and healing. I have seen over and over again that, in our final days of life, the only thing that matters is people. And in a healthy situation, at the moment of death, the only thing left in the room is love.

Love seems to be the answer to so many deep questions. When asked to define God, many people will say, "God is Love." When asked what the purpose of life is many people will say, "To give and receive love." What can break your heart? Love. When asked what the greatest gift you can receive is, many will say, "Unconditional love." What can heal our broken world? Love. What matters most when you take your final breath? Love.

Even in the horrific conditions of the concentration camp, Viktor Frankl was able to find fulfillment when he thought about his beloved wife. He had no idea where she was or under what conditions she was living, and he hoped that she was in better circumstances than he. At that time he was stripped away of everything. To his captors he was simply Number 119,104.

As he contemplated about his love for his beloved wife, Frankl wrote, "A thought transfixed me: for the first time in my life I saw the truth as it is set into song by so many poets, proclaimed as the final wisdom by so many thinkers. The truth – that love is the ultimate and the highest goal to which man can aspire. Then I grasped the meaning of the greatest secret that human poetry and human thought and belief have to impart: The salvation of man is through love and in love. I understood how a man who has nothing left in this world may still know bliss, be it only for a brief moment, in the contemplation of his beloved." They took everything they could from him. But, as it was with his attitude, they could not touch his heart or his soul.

A Little More About Unfinished Business

If you have a burning desire to do something, do it. If you have a burning need to say something, say it. It's part of keeping ourselves clear and peaceful. Harboring unfinished business is toxic. Some people can't even let go to die peacefully if they have something left unsaid or undone. I've seen it. Something that may have been handled decades before with a simple phone call or a hug suddenly becomes urgent and chaotic. And sometimes it's too late.

After September 11th was forever etched into our psyche, lots of people changed how they prioritize their lives, how they plan their days and how they express themselves. Rather than cleaning the house and then calling your friend or visiting a sick neighbor, people started calling their friends or visiting their sick neighbors and then cleaning the house. After 9-11, love and relationships trumped clean laundry, as it should.

Every month or so, it's a good idea to take stock of your emotional state and review the dynamics of your personal relationships. It's like cleaning house, but on the inside. Don't store up your worries, your comments, your advice, your compliments or your love for the perfect time in the future to dole them out. Don't even store up the hard stuff to say. It matters, too.

Towards the end of life, people often engage themselves and their loved ones in a life review. This is often a joyous walk down memory lane, where stories are shared from weddings and births and travel and parties and life's big moments, but it usually also involves a reminiscing of the little routines that made their life different from everyone else's. Simple memories like eating dinner outside, family traditions, inside jokes, some meal that the family shared, or a hike they all enjoyed together. Sometimes a life review consists of some hard stuff, too, like loss, grief, broken-heartedness, loneliness, missed opportunities, mistakes and regrets. Often this is where the unfinished business comes in. If you are given the privilege to be sitting with a person who is reviewing their life, listen well. It is an honor.

To avoid the build-up of unfinished business at the end of your life, ask yourself from time to time who needs to hear you say one of these words:

"Thank you."
"I'm sorry. Will you forgive me?"
"I forgive you."
"I love you."
Tell them now. That way, in the end you will only need to say "goodbye."

Stories About Love and Relationships

The Things We Do For Love

I have gone to great lengths to impress a man before, but this one takes the cake, or should I say pie. While I am deeply sorry for my lack of honesty, I am still able to giggle when I think about it. Besides, I did not give chicken broth to a vegetarian or eggs to a vegan. So I did not cause any harm...

More Confessions
Home-Baked Fresh Pumpkin Pie

It was the day before Thanksgiving and I was nestled into a mountainside home in Carmel Valley. I was visiting my then boyfriend, Tom, who in ways was sometimes more like a teacher or mentor to me than a boyfriend. He lived with this carefree attitude of generosity and abundance, never really worrying about where his next dollar would come from because he "trusted the universe would provide." I thought that was bullshit but then every time he ran out of money the fricking universe would give him some cash and prove me wrong. One time he was almost broke and he spent $200.00 on an iron. I literally went insane. He would iron his shirts like he was the Sultan of Brunei or something and I know for sure he just loved watching me seethe with irritation and disbelief every time he took it out. Just to bother me, he cradled it like it was a warm adorable house cat and then would sing songs while he ironed.

The reason he was like a teacher to me is because he embodied all the things that I had not yet learned how to be. He was confident, entrepreneurial, very disciplined, and he went after what he wanted like a shark on steroids. Oh, and did I mention the fact that he was extremely healthy? Not healthy like a normal vegetarian or a Paleo person or someone who goes to Weight Watchers or tries to avoid dairy, gluten and sugar. No, this was decades ago and he was in a category all of his own. Soon I found myself eating brown rice mochi instead of bread and cringing every time I had to gag down another unfamiliar meal.

The day before Thanksgiving was a glorious, crisp day. Friends were coming the next day and I only had one task while Tom was out running all the errands. He knew I loved to bake so he asked me to make the homemade pumpkin pie. This sounded achievable and that way I was able to avoid making the miso gravy and the tempeh stuffing.

So off I went to the store to gather the supplies, including the fresh pumpkin. This was my first time using fresh pumpkin, so I called all my friends for advice and of course none of them had any, so I was dependent on the earthy, new age cookbooks on Tom's kitchen counter.

I prepared and baked the pumpkin and the house smelled heavenly, but later when I pulled it out it looked and smelled worse than baby poop. It was watery and slimy and nothing close to the pumpkin that comes perfectly out of a can. So I did what any independent and resourceful woman would do. I got in my car and drove to a "normal" grocery store, where I bought two large cans of 100% pureed pumpkin.

I quickly ran home, opened the cans and poured the canned pumpkin mixture into a bowl. In order to hide the evidence, I filled the two empty cans with the pumpkin poop mixture, grabbed a small shovel and got in my car. I drove up his property around the back where I would not be spotted in case Tom came home early. There, I dug a deep hole where I buried the two cans and then even covered them with twigs and leaves.

I rushed home and finished mixing the ingredients. I got the pies in the oven and was just tidying up when Tom pulled into the driveway. He walked in, smiled and said, "Wow, that pie smells delicious. The entire house smells like Thanksgiving. I can't wait to eat it."

He asked for a second serving of pie and I gladly passed it to him as the visual of those cans buried on the hill put a big smile on my face.

On Loving Yourself

Love takes may forms. There is romantic love, a parent's love, and love between friends, which is one of my favorites. I can't imagine life without my girlfriends. There is also love for humanity, love for the planet, and love for our animals. But it all starts with self-love. If you don't love yourself, it's hard to love someone else.

Try to remember what you looked like when you were a young child, about four to seven years old, hopefully before the world got to you and polluted you with messages of self-doubt and inadequacy. Underneath the protective layers, you are still that young person. You are more than adequate. You were created to fit into the seasons and the stars and the gravitational pull that holds you tethered to the earth. Without you, the ripple effect would be felt around the world, from the inside of your home, to your work place and your favorite grocery store. It would create a shift that stretches to China and

Ethiopia and the cornfields in Iowa. That is how much you matter.

Love others. Love well and fully. But love yourself first.

Walking Towards Home

It was so simple.
I was free.
No armor and no judgment.
I laughed uncontrollably
and chased butterflies.

Years passed.
The world screamed my name.
It screamed, and sometimes
Gently whispered for me to come.

Following without contemplation, I left.
And the world pushed, and pulled.
It shook and it twisted me.
It loved me, hurt me, held me
And laughed at me.

Today, in the whirlwind of my story,
I turned around
And there she was…

The young, curious girl
Standing in the distance
With outstretched arms…

She is love and grace and
Kindness and simplicity.
She is fearless and strong
And ready to venture out.

How could I have left her there
So many years ago?

Bowing in gratitude for second chances,
I stop running away and,
Being true to myself,
I walk towards home.

Friendship Redefined

To me, friendship is still when you roll up in a ball on your best friend's bed and laugh until you almost pee. It's that safe place to cry and know that you will not be judged or misunderstood. It's the people that know everything about you, and love you anyway. Those are your "true north" type of friends who are there in sickness and in health, for better or for worse, for richer and for poorer until death do we part. They are priceless.

Today the word friend has been diluted down to include people that you have never even met before. It makes me sad and nostalgic. There was a time when Carly had more Facebook friends than I had hairs on my head. I get it that the accumulation of "friends" is a status symbol of the younger generation. It screams out, "I'm somebody special. I know lots of people who love me and think I'm cool!" I get that. But is also means, "I say yes to anyone who wants to be my friend. I want to look cool, even if I'm not."

Once I challenged Carly to go through her entire list of "friends" and delete anyone she didn't know. The list shrunk by about 20% in minutes. Then, I challenged her to delete anyone on her list of "friends" that she could not tell me at least two facts about. It could be anything, like how she met them, where they go to school, or where they live. Just two facts. Well, that exercise soon became known as "the great purging" because her list of "friends" dropped by another 50% or so! The good news is that her "friend" list is now more authentic and real and not filled with people who just happened upon her. She chooses them.

So, on behalf of Carly and all the other kids out there searching for your authentic self in the midst of social media madness, I would like to propose "National Deletion Day," where everyone takes an hour to prune their list of "friends" down to fit this definition:

FRIEND: A person attached to another by feelings of affection and personal regard. A person you respect and trust.

Another way of thinking about friendship, which I personally relate to, was written by an unknown author, "Friendship isn't about those who you have known the longest. It's about those who came and never left your side." That is a perfect example of showing up and finishing well.

Deb and me, best friends through thick and thin.

More on Friendship
"The Coat"

From my chemo journal:

When we got to the airport on Christmas Eve, I thought a week of traveling might have been a BIG mistake. I heard people making comments about me because I was bald, looking at me, and I even heard one woman tell her husband how sad it was that I had such young children. On the plane, I felt like a different person...dressed in my glasses, matching cancer hat and medical mask. No one would have recognized me and I hardly recognized myself. It was an odd, self-conscious, "poor me" kind of feeling that I hate. I felt misunderstood and judged somehow by my appearance.

But then we landed and everything was perfect. Christmas was a wonderful week with family and friends on the beach in Santa Cruz, California. Love and friendship took away any traces of toxic cancer blues. The good days out-number the bad by far, and even the bad ones don't really change my life or who I am.

What I've learned these past few weeks is that, like childbirth, the pain and discomfort from cancer and chemotherapy fade away and I can enjoy my life. God gave us our minds and the ability to remember, but somehow embedded in there is also the ability to emotionally forget! God is so smart.

My entire family feels humbled and privileged to have such wonderful people in our lives. Our friends added so much to our already full hearts and I think that's why I recovered more quickly this time. The chemo chemicals were different and should be better for the next 2 months of treatment, but I think it's been our family and friends that have really lifted me up and carried me through these past few weeks. And the beach in Santa Cruz…And, how could I ever forget…the coat.

Thank God for the coat. That was the day I remembered how much I love to laugh. I don't mean a little chuckle. I mean that rip-roaring, belly-aching, I don't care who is looking kind of laugh. Girlfriend's laughing together is the best. One day three of my closest friends and I went shopping. I will protect their names by the unbreakable girlfriend code of silence, except now that enough time has gone by I will call the main character in this story Erin Murrows, another perfect rhyme. Erin Murrows found a coat she loved in a store and told us all about it…it was soft, knee-length, casual and perfect for business meetings. And it was on sale. She went on and on about this coat until she almost ran out of breath, and then told us there was only one problem. It didn't fit. It was too small.

We all agreed that it didn't fit. But Erin Murrows loved it, noting that it looked fabulous from the back and it was about 70% off. How could anyone turn that down…even if it didn't fit? She REALLY wanted it. My friends, Liz and Reggie, agreed that she will need to stand facing the wall wherever she goes since the coat only fits in the back. Liz suggested that we look for a matching pair of pants that don't zip and shoes that are too small to make the coat seem just right. So the four of us were rolling around laughing our guts out in the middle of Neiman Marcus, me with my bald head and cancer hat, not exactly a fashion statement! We were hysterical. We went on and on and could not stop. It was the first time in three months my stomach hurt from laughing, and not from cancer.

That night I started thinking about my goals for the New Year. I became inspired to live a fuller, deeper, richer, and simpler life, in community with others. I want to spend time with the people I love, heal my body, and remember to laugh as hard as I did the day Erin Murrows bought a coat that didn't fit.

be still

That Girl in My Tribe

A woman learns that the lump is cancer and her battle begins. Her friends support her as her breasts are taken from her and her femininity washes down the drain with her hair and her immortality, yet she is strong.

I am that girl, and you are that girl, for you are in my

tribe. And that means that when I hurt, you hurt. But then, the tide of life turns and when I love, you love and when I rejoice, then you too shall rejoice.

A friend grieves and aches as her family slowly falls apart. Her husband does not see her, or her beauty. He sits disconnected, as the proverbial house of cards crumbles around him, and she is scared, yet she is strong.

You are that girl, and I am that girl, for you are in my tribe. And when you hurt, I hurt. But then, the tide of life turns and when you love, I love and when you rejoice, then I too shall rejoice.

A young girl is behind the wheel one fateful night. Suddenly a terrible accident changes everything. One young girl is lost, another young girl must carry the very heavy burden on her shoulders, and she is sad and broken, yet she is strong.

Your daughter is that girl, you are that girl, and I am that girl, too, for you are in my tribe. And when she hurts, then you hurt, and I hurt, too. But then, the tide of life turns and when she loves, we love and when she rejoices, then we too shall rejoice again.

Priceless

We knew a loving family in Tennessee with three teenage daughters. It was the youngest daughter's sixteenth birthday and her parents wanted to get her something special. Their oldest daughter had recently celebrated a major milestone birthday and they splurged a bit and bought her something bigger and grander than was normal for their family. For their youngest daughter's sixteenth birthday, they decided to surprise her with a cello, which she had wanted for a long time.

During the celebration, when it came time to open gifts, the family was all gathered around the young daughter as she excitedly opened her beautiful gift. It was at that moment that the sweet mom looked up and noticed tears in her middle child's eyes. These were subtle tears and the mom could see that her daughter was trying her best to hold them back, but these are looks that a mother recognizes in an instant.

Later that evening, the parents were alone in the kitchen with their middle daughter. They asked her if everything was OK, and their daughter broke down and cried. She told her mom and dad that she was sorry that she was feeling this way, but that she was noticing that her older sister got a special gift on her big birthday, and her younger sister had just been given an exquisite cello for her birthday, but when she had recently turned 18, she was given a simple necklace that may have cost only $30 or so. Clearly, this is not a selfish girl and she felt embarrassed to be feeling the way she did.

The mom was devastated and felt awful for the way her daughter was feeling. She began wondering what she could do to "fix" the situation. What could she buy her? What did she want? What could she give her that would make her feel special, too?

While she was busy thinking of the perfect gift, her husband told the middle daughter to get her shoes on and get in the car because the two of them were going out. The mom spent the whole time they were gone wondering what gift her husband was going to buy for her middle daughter. She wondered how much he would spend and worried that he would spend more than they could afford.

A few hours later they came home. Her daughter was in a very happy mood and told her mom that this was one of the best days of her life. The mom became progressively worried about how much this was all going to add up to, but she kissed her child goodnight without asking for all the details and went to find her husband.

"What did you get her that made her so happy?" the mom asked.

Her husband said, "Oh, I didn't get her anything. I took her out to dinner and I looked her in the eyes and I told her how proud I am of her. I told her about holding her the day she was born, and watching her play in the yard when she was a sweet, little girl. I told her about how much my life has changed because of her and how much joy she has brought our family. I told her how proud I am of her character, how much I enjoy her kind spirit and how I think she has grown up to be such a strong and beautiful woman. I explained to her that she is priceless and more valuable than any gift I could ever buy."

"Then we finished dinner and came home."

Unconventional Love

We all have a story. A story about how we met our best friend. A story about how we decided where to go to college, and a story about how we met our first love and then, for most of us the story of how we fell in love with the next person and then the next person. All stories that lead us to today. All different. All meaningful.

In my day I have been through my share of love stories. There was Mr. Bike through the Marin County rolling hills, and then there was Mr. Fancy Pants who tried to make me look like his trophy date. That guy had a hard job because that title did not come easy to me. Then there was Mr. Exercise, and Mr. Technology, and for a short stint there was the relentless Dr. Pee, who judged my attractiveness and breeding potential by the flow patterns in my urine. Obviously that one didn't work out.

One time I dated a guy who seemed promising. We had a wonderful first date, with lots of laughter, which is always a good sign for me. The second date started off well and we were enjoying a glass of wine at sunset when he commented that I was wearing the exact same pair of socks I was wearing on our first date the week before. Bye Bye, Mr. Sock Man.

Since I don't really know what I am doing with all of these life stories and notes I have accumulated, and also because I may be dead when someone reads this, I can be absolutely truthful about my desire to have an affair behind my husband's back. After all, I'm only human. So, I look at handsome men and I think, wow, it sure would be fun to have someone like him to sit around and laugh hysterically with, to have deep intimate conversations with, and to go on exotic vacations with. I dream, and I fantasize, and all of that lasts somewhere between five to eight seconds, depending on my day.

After that, I quickly move on to thought number two, which is the following: Truth is, I have a pretty awesome husband and I never want to be in a twisted complex affair. It sounds like way too much work! And even if I were single, I don't think I would ever want to cook and clean up after another man or group of people of any size ever again. Besides, there is no one I could ever imagine being with that would give me more of the things that truly matter than Mark.

But that is such a boring story, so here's the real ending. If anything ever happens to Mark, I am going to have an affair with our neighbor, Carlos. Well, it won't be a traditional full-on affair. You see, I am just going to have an affair with his voice. He has the sexiest voice in the world. He always sounds like he just had sex outside and I am sure he is always walking around his house in nothing but a towel.

If Mark dies, I am going to ask him to call me on occasion and just say something mildly romantic in his deep, sexy Italian voice and I will keep it forever on my answering machine. Whenever I get lonely, I will just listen to my messages. Oh, and I have a back up plan. Carlos is an eye surgeon, so if I'm too chicken to ask him to call me, I'll call him about a terribly irritating eye infection. I'm sure he will call me back with that same sexy voice and say, "Hi Diane, it's Carlos. I'm calling to tell you that you have a sty in your right eye," but it will be all dramatic sounding and beautiful like a song. That is all I need. And I will keep it forever.

Karmic Footnote: Be careful what you ask for. Since I wrote this story, I have had exactly three terribly irritating, long-lasting eye infections, each including the dreaded sty in, you guessed it, my right eye!

be still

Jesus in the House

Like most mama bears, I love my kids to the end of the earth and back. My whole family is the magnetic pull in my internal compass. My husband is my rock. And I love my friends with a fiery passion because I chose them and they chose me to walk side by side together through green pastures of joy and through dark jungles of uncertainty, too. With a heart filled with more love than I could have ever imagined possible, I must admit that these people all bug the shit out of me sometimes, too. And I'm sure this feeling goes both ways. We are perfectly imperfect.

And I love Jesus, too. Now this may come as a shock to some, like those same friends and acquaintances who long ago called out for the salvation police to save my lost and ragged soul. But I do. Jesus is the bomb. He gets me and I get him. And we don't have any of the same drama and issues that I have going on with everyone else in my life. It's an awesome relationship, really.

Recently I realized why my relationship with Jesus is so different than my relationship with everyone else. I thought it was because well, you know, Jesus was perfect and all that, but then I realized that isn't it at all. The reason I don't have any of those issues with Jesus is because he isn't here! He doesn't live in my house. There is nothing to get upset with him about.

But if he were here, I wonder, what would Jesus do? Would Jesus leave his robe and boxer shorts in a pile on his bedroom floor? Would Jesus be resistant to brushing and flossing? Would Jesus blast his music really loud and talk to people on social media in his bedroom rather than hanging with the family? And what would Jesus do for exercise? Does Jesus even know how to swim? I can't imagine him in a bathing suit. I also can't imagine him playing football or baseball, although I think he might be quite good at basketball. I'll bet he would love to get all cozy in a pair of sweat pants and a warm, fuzzy hoodie before he celebrated his birthday on Christmas morning.

If Jesus were living in my house, he would be another mouth to feed and another human to take care of. He would know for sure that he was welcome, loved and belonged here forever. And I'm sure if Jesus was living in the house, he would bug me sometimes, too. Even if he was "perfect" he would irritate me because I generally am not attracted to "perfect."

So that settles it. Living with humans, even if it was Jesus, isn't easy. I'm going to start lighting a candle every morning in my house, just as a reminder that it isn't Jesus in the house, but the essence and spirit of Jesus in the house, that keeps our hearts open, loving and united.

Show Up and Finish Well

CHAPTER 8 AND 1/2

Showing Up For Your Children

Before I can love you, I have to love me. Before I know you, I have to know me.

Who I am

I am the little girl who puts her arm in a tree and lets bees cover her with no fear, who giggles at riddle books she reads by candlelight in bed at night, and the little girl who plays the same song over and over again on a well-worn record player.

I am the teenager who awkwardly parts her hair and then brushes it forward to cover most of her face, the teenager who is afraid to try out for teams, who diets on M&M's and who finds out the hard way that

Brussels sprouts do not flush.

I am the fresh-faced, confident, young entrepreneur with a successful career, yet who also is so self-conscious and insecure that she frequently cancels dates because of pimples and carries a dictionary in her purse when she dates intelligent men who use big words.

I am the young adult who runs the water so people can't hear her pee, and the one who puts her spices in alphabetical order, has all labels facing forward and usually falls in love with the underdog.

I am the wife who respects her husbands deep sense of integrity and feels like the luckiest woman in the world, but I am also the one who flips him off sometimes when he's not looking and makes fun of how he shuffles like an old man and walks like a duck.

I am the mom who tries to provide my kids with unconditional love and an authentic worldview, so they realize that life does not always greet them at the door with a bouquet of milk chocolate roses. But I am also the mom who barks like an insane hound dog trying to get them out the door in the morning.

I am the one who secretly ponders weird things on airplanes and other public places. I'm the one wondering who on the plane has traveled the most, who has eaten the most pizza, who has the most hair follicles, who has had the most sex and who has committed the worst crime.

I am the silly one who tells kids inappropriate things for fun and memories. I tell Jack that his penis may burn and shrivel and he may be unable to have kids if he doesn't put a pillow, in our house affectionately referred to as a "penis-protector" between the computer and his crotch. (I must also someday apologize for telling him that Spam was made out of ground body parts, like ALL body parts, so he wouldn't eat it.)

I am the aging woman, feeling inwardly as if the wisdom of the years has given me compassion, empathy, strength, awareness and an understanding of what it means to cultivate and nurture joy in everyday life to the extent that I am capable of. But I am also a sagging bag of flab. I have brown dot-to-dot spots on my skin from chemo or too much fun in the sun when I was younger. I have wrinkles that are becoming more and more reminiscent of the roadmap of life's journey...the same etched wrinkles that I used to stare at on my grandmother's face when I was a little girl.

It is all part of my story.

Who I am Not

I am not Maya Angelou, whose words pull you right into her soul.

I am not Mother Teresa. Not even close.

I am not Mother Mary, even though Jack wondered if he were the Baby Jesus.

I am not Dr. Brene Brown, whose carefully researched scientific formulas and statistics provide an undeniable titanium backbone for her every bit of advice.

And I am not Anne Lamott, who we all love so much for how she wears her hilarious twisted heart on her sleeve and uses her life to enhance ours.

And I am definitely not Oprah, though somehow I feel I know her well.

But I love these women and so many more. And I am sure that, over the years, nuggets of wisdom and significance from their words have impacted mine. So in a sense, I am every woman. We give and take and learn and grow from each other.

I am so grateful for the influence of so many amazing women in my life, from Maya Angelou to my neighbor Kathy, who makes lilikoi jelly and granola bars and passes them out to all of us just because she loves us. I am blessed.

Who You Are

I have always loved you.

Before I saw your beautiful face, I saw the ripple of your tiny footprints pressing from inside my tummy. I loved you even then and knew that you were a miracle.

The pain of childbirth came and went, immediately replaced by the indescribable joy that filled every corner of my heart the moment I held you in my arms. You are a round, smiling bundle of sweetness. You ask for what you want through smiles and tears and everything in between. I spoke your language before you ever spoke a word.

You are cuddly and free. You dance. You are free from worries and the world is a small, safe playground made especially for you and your little friends. You smell like springtime.

You are every child. You are your best friend, your neighbor and the kids who live in the next town. You are growing and becoming aware that the world is bigger than your playground, and even learning that it isn't always safe or fair. But you dance. And you smell like summer.

You are unique. You are you. You are a feeling, intricate, and thoughtful being. You are walking with others, but you are also walking alone. You are paving your own path and learning to water your own garden. Your world is growing even bigger. Sometimes you sense fear and sometimes life just doesn't make sense. And soon comes fall.

You discover that people can be mean. Life can be hard. You find your safe spots and you learn that sometimes it feels better to hide. Yet you are strong and you know that the place of wisdom comes from being the observer. You don't always need to participate. Stand back and wait. For it is winter.

And now you are off to college. Your story is your own now, and I stand in the road watching you pull away with your car packed to the brim with all that represents the first few chapters of your life.

As you turn the corner, all the emotions that I have ever felt because of knowing you are building up into one giant tear in the corner of my eye. I wave goodbye and watch you turn and drive away. I gently whisper, "Don't forget to dance."

You wave back, hair blowing in the wind. The tear drops to the ground. And it is springtime again.

On Family

My friend Theresa tells her kids, "I know I didn't do everything perfectly, but I want you to know that I always tried my best." That's it. That's all that we can do. Warts and all, we try our best and then our kids grow up and go off to live the lives that they create for themselves.

It happened to each of us, too. We were raised by people who were products of the parenting they received themselves. They likely cannot love you well if they were not loved themselves. It is a generational cyclone. But in the end, it is your life, and your journey. I think we should all stop blaming our parents for the bad stuff. It's a tether to the inadequacies of our ancestors, and a ball and chain around our ankles that keeps us from the freedom of moving forward. It's time to move on without the mean, little editor sitting on our shoulder reiterating every negative thing we were told or taught when we were little. Flick that jerky editor off your shoulder now! You are good enough, smart enough, capable enough, beautiful enough, strong enough, creative, happy, and deserving enough. And not only that, you are more than enough!

I love my family a ton, but I seriously don't know how I ended up with this particular bunch of people. We are a tiny, mixed-bag sort of family where no one is even remotely alike. We're like when you open the top drawer in your kitchen that's filled with a little of this and a little of that. You can find almost anything in that drawer, from tape and scissors to reading glasses, and maybe a compass, a hairbrush and a slinky. That's us. A bit of everything. There are lots of stories in my family, some of which I believe remain untold. I guess we would call those secrets, if we were going to admit that they even exist. I do love these wackos, but I don't really see myself in any one of them.

Occasionally I ask my mom, "Are you really my mother?" She laughs and fully knows that I am making a joke tinged with a hint of serious pondering. I usually ask this when she can't make up her mind what she wants to eat, when she refuses to stand up for herself, or when she's doing the Pursitis thing.

I'm sure we are all related, but sometimes I think I have more in common with the skeletons in their closets. I can't wait to meet them someday.

Thing is, no matter how different we are, we've managed to accumulate a lifetime of memories and experiences together. Some of my favorite childhood memories are weekends spent with our little speed boat, the Dee Dee Pooh. I can't remember what I had for dinner last night, but I can remember perfectly that the license number for that boat was CF 4794 CB. I think all those positive memories helped imprint that number in my mind.

The best times happened on Lake Tahoe, where water temperature averages about 50 degrees at the surface so lots of people find it too cold to swim, but my brother and I loved it. I remember being huddled in the hull with him, nauseous and bouncing insanely over choppy waters after a full day of waterskiing.

I've been told many times about the day my mom took me out on the boat with my Aunt Toni when I was a little girl. Apparently, I was holding some kind of a floatie and I started drifting away. My mom and Aunt Toni apparently had a lengthy discussion about who should "have to jump in and save me." The story goes that they decided that neither of them was willing to jump into the icy water, so they used their loud voices and encouraging words to finally reconnect me with the boat.

One night, when I was a teenager, a strong, windy storm came through Lake Tahoe. We could hear the Dee Dee Pooh knocking up against the dock. It was pitch black outside when my dad said that he was going to have to move the boat, tie it to a buoy and swim back to the dock. I offered to help him, and even though he was reluctant, he knew he needed me. It was a challenge to get the boat out there, and no fun at all jumping into that ice cold water to get back to shore. But my dad was so proud of me. I can remember the look in his eyes when we were done, and I loved hearing him tell the story over and over again. I felt like a super hero!

The Power of Choice

One of my favorite topics to talk to kids about is what I call "The Power of Choice." I start by asking them how many think that their parents make most of the decisions in their lives. They almost all raise their hands and grumble. They feel like parents, teachers and adults in general are always telling them what to do. They say they don't have a lot of freedom or opportunity to make decisions on their own, which makes them feel incapable and childish. My task is to help them see that they actually choose a lot more than they think they do. They are in the process of becoming their own person, and with that comes more responsibility, and also more freedom and more choices. Everyone is stunned when I tell them that statistic that we make about 612 calculated decisions every single day!

In smaller groups we talk about ways to better know themselves, tools for healthy communication, family dynamics, peer pressure, and avoiding drugs and alcohol. We also talk about choosing friends and activities, and I always make sure to squeeze in the changes in our world due to technology. This wraps up well with choosing your friends, because for many of these kids, their primary relationships are with their phones and laptops. Their social lives take place primarily alone in their bedroom, although they don't really ever feel alone anymore because everyone they know is just a click away. I'm not sure we will ever get away from this new relationship model, but I'm not going down easily on this one. There is no substitute for fresh air, eye contact and a human hug.

I might tell the kids, "Your words are powerful. They can be weapons if used in an unkind way. For example, have you ever had someone tell you a secret that was really just gossip? Well, that person made a decision to gossip, but you also made a decision. Did you agree and gossip back? Did you laugh? Did you stick up for the person that was gossiped about, did you walk away, or did you tell the person you don't like gossip? Maybe you said nothing at all, but that was still a choice. And your parents were not even there. This is how powerful you already are."

Within an hour, they are empowered because they realize that, even that very day they made choices. They decided what socks to wear, what to say, how they feel and respond, what to do, where to go, where they would sit in class, who they wanted to hang out with and more. And it feels good.

We also talk about what they do for fun, and WHY they do it. It's common to ask a kid, "What to you like to do when you aren't at school?" But if you really want to get to know your kids, ask them "why do you do that?" Or "why do you want to do that?" Asking powerful, open-ended questions fosters communication with your child and forces them to go a little deeper.

Perhaps there is a two-fold lesson here because, at the core, I like to show the kids just how many choices they make every day. But lots of their progress and growth comes when parents are willing to let go to give kids the chance to discover their own power. I encourage all kids to:

Choose activities that bring you joy.

Choose what you stand for.

Choose friends you can trust and who will support what you stand for.

Choose an adult or a mentor who you can talk to.

Choose to honor your feelings – "Feel it to heal it!"

Choose to pause and "Own Your Space" before you respond.

Choose to "Just Say No" and then don't leave the door open!

Like Eleanor Roosevelt said "I am who I am today because of the choices I made yesterday."

God sent Jesus to teach all of us imperfect people, and I'm pretty sure God also sent other representatives to help with some other very important tasks around the world. They are called parents, and they have a hard job, so they were given an extra dose of love when they first met the people they care for. They needed it so they could handle the turning tides. We also call these people aunties, uncles, grandparents, and friends. God is omnipresent. That's His thing. But He could not physically be in every single household all the time, so he entrusted these beautiful treasures called children into the care of their parents.

In the beginning, God created these helpless, dependent beings and made them as adorable as can be so that the parents simply melted and fell in love. This love grew into the most glorious bond ever known to mankind. As the children grew, God gave them words, and smiles, and arms for hugging, and bodies that love to cuddle and the parents melted even more.

Then God gave them a sense of wonder, and friends,

and a growing intellect and little tastes of independence.

And then God gave them acne. This was the beginning of the decline. Along came self-absorption, attitude, and a supreme desire to detach from all things related to parents. This may include signs on the bedroom door that say, "Stay Out of MY room" as if they actually own their rooms. It may also include rudeness, acting disrespectful, and spontaneously lashing out, followed immediately by requests for money, food, or rides to the mall.

I fully understand that children did not pick these parents, their school, their house, their religion, or their underwear. So maybe they have a right to be a little pissed off. These parents, who they didn't even pick, are telling them what to do, eat, wear, say, and are forming their happy, fun-loving brains into walking, talking college applications. That kind of sucks for them. And it kind of sucks for the parents too, because they become like a concierge service, catering to the needs of the teen so the child can graduate from the "A" factory and leave their parents in the dust for Harvard or Stanford or some tiny school in the middle of Fargo, North Dakota. It's making some sense to me now. Of course they want to get the hell away from these parents. Wouldn't you? It seems as if almost every kid I know wants to go as far away from home as possible.

Sometimes I wonder what would happen if I just lightened up a bit? Let the kids relax and have more down time. Let them fall down so they will learn how to get back up. Let them flex their independence-seeking muscles, but make sure they are safe. Give them an allowance and stick to it, so their silly purchases are up to them, not me. Let them feel disappointment, boredom, and loneliness. Let them make decisions, too, for all of this is part of life. I'm sure I would be surprised and impressed by what they could do if I just got out of the way!

Kids and "Things"

While we often count our money and our things, and guard over our possessions because we OWN them, it is healthy to remember a few simple truths. First off, it's the people who matter, not the things. You were born into this world naked and without any possessions whatsoever. Like all of us, you have likely accumulated a storehouse of riches, including money, cars, a house, jewelry and other sometimes even less valuable items that you cherish. Having things and caring about our possessions if fine, but we must not lose sight of the fact that we will die in the exact fashion that we entered the world, naked and without any possessions whatsoever.

185

In addition, God is the creator of you and me and everything that exists. Psalm 24:1 says, "The earth is the Lord's, and everything in it, the world and all who live in it." Everything is really borrowed, on loan from the Creator of the universe. So it's not really ours, but we get attached to our stuff. That's why the bible also says it is harder for a rich man to get into heaven than it is for a camel to pass through the eye of a needle. The love, desire and quest for money is for many, the root of evil.

It's not so much that things that we treasure on earth are bad for us. It is just that they are not lasting. They do not lead to eternal joy. I have been actively pursuing a more simple life. As I read that, I feel like a hypocrite as we are remodeling and working to improve our home. But what I'm talking about is the stuff. The piles in the garage, the storage shed, and the boxes that have not been touched for 15 years.

There was a period of time on our street when there were lots of break-ins and things were getting stolen. I was getting frustrated and wanted to move away, but then I had an idea. I will rid my home of possessions that I value. I will create a home that can be robbed so I no longer have to worry about losing my "stuff." That started my "lightening our load" crusade. Just keep it simple, and replaceable. Part of this crusade included what I labeled "inventory control." Every time anyone got something new, something old would be discarded. No wonder my kids think I'm nuts.

Oh, no. Here comes another embarrassing but true confession. Unfortunately for the kids, I took this "lightening our load" crusade to great heights. When I was in my twenties, I had a sweet Little Sister named Mira from the Big Brothers/Big Sisters program. We hiked, shared meals, went to fairs and had tons of fun together. She is now grown up and married, and I am so in awe of her beauty and grace and who she has become.

Because of Mira, I always call Big Brothers/Big Sisters to donate items for resale and for those in need. Somehow I always get into a slightly obsessive compulsive groove when I know they are coming. First, I get online and schedule a pick-up, even though I haven't collected anything to donate. You have to tell Big Brothers/Big Sister if you want to donate 1-3 bags, 4-10 bags, or more. I always chose 4-10 bags. That gives me the challenge.

Then, when the house is quiet and I am alone for a few hours, I grab a giant black, plastic garbage bag and go from room to room finding things to give away. Our house is tiny, there are only two bedrooms and five of us were living in it until Carly left for college. Jack slept in a part of the living room with his drum set. So we really didn't have space to accumulate. I would go into the kid's room and start with clothes they had outgrown. Inevitably I would find toys that have not been touched for years and books that would be better suited for younger children. And I would not stop until I filled at least 4 plastic bags. I don't know why, but it felt so good.

One day when Carly was young, she was looking for an old, rubber doll and said to me, "Mom have you seen Betty Spaghetti?"

"No, Carly, I haven't seen her in awhile," I responded in truth because clearly I had not seen her lately.

"Well, do you know where she is, mom?"

"No, I really have no idea," I said. And that was true as well. I did not know where Betty was. Besides, I didn't have the heart to tell her that Betty Spaghetti was probably either living in some other kids house or buried at the bottom of a landfill in Kansas or something.

I always dreaded the next question so I would scurry out looking all mom-style busy so she wouldn't ask me to help her find her or worse yet, ask me if I threw her away.

Sorry, Carly.

Back to Gibran

It's an honor that people call me often to talk through relationship problems, mostly involving their teenagers. I always try to help after I chuckle a bit. I don't really know they call me because I would probably be better at Olympic pole-vaulting than I am at parenting. It's so hard. I have had more than my share of hard stuff in the parenting arena. As I write this, a dim light bulb is flickering in the distance, helping me see why actually they do call. It's the arena. I jump in, even for the hard stuff. For teenagers sometimes it really does feel like a rodeo, with the teenager being the bucking bronco that we are attempting to calm and settle just enough for them to hit the pause button and recalibrate.

I don't have the answers and God knows there are so many different choices to be made in the parenting arena. But I am not afraid to show up, for my own kid's stuff, and my friend's kids, too.

Once Carly went through times of low self-esteem and self-destructive behavior that got so bad that we couldn't handle it. She ended up in a wilderness program for teens where her therapist, Dr. Fred, an angel on earth, taught her that, "The whirlwind of your own drama is your greatest obstacle." And he was right. With time, she shined and became a leader and owned her patterns. It was truly beautiful, but watching Carly walk away into the winter wilderness, knowing that she was going to spend a couple of months outdoors in the harsh, cold mountains in Colorado sleeping on a tarp in the snow was the hardest moment of my life. I might as well of been holding a flashing neon sign that said, "I suck as a mom. I can't raise my own child. I need you to do it for me."

The cool part of the wilderness story was that there were so many life lessons in there for both of us. For me, I asked for help when I needed it. And I realized that my village of friends and support was both deep and wide and would never let us fall too hard. For Carly, she learned to see herself in a new, healthier way and she learned that she is a survivor and that she can do hard things. We all grew up and our family dynamic started to change.

People say they have to sacrifice so much to be a parent but I don't see it only like that. Well, it's true. It is a gigantic sacrifice and sometimes I want to run away from the endless, smelly laundry pile and drown myself in a hot bath filled with a gallon of organic coconut oil. And sometimes I want to leave for a whole year and make them miss me and appreciate all that I do. But then there is the other side, and when I am in that happy place, the walls around my tired heart crumble down and I remember how important we are to these young kids.

So I start another load of laundry, wipe the milk off the kitchen counter and open my heart to why so many of us do this crazy thing called parenting anyway. The truth is, I feel it is a privilege to be linked with another human being who magnifies my soul and changes how I live my life and impacts how I am connected to the planet today as well as tomorrow. It is an honor to love someone so much that I hurt when they hurt and I smile simply because they are smiling. But I don't want to be a drone, hovering over my kids just waiting for them to screw up so I can jump in and rescue them. Not cool. How did I get to that point in the first place? It felt like love, but I'm pretty sure it was fear.

When I was a hippie the book that was by my bedside for almost a decade was "The Prophet" by Kahlil Gibran. His poetic perspective on love, friendship, suffering, marriage and life captured my curiosity. At that point, I was not even sure I wanted to have children. But when I read Gibran's words about children I thought that if I ever did have a child, I would parent with Gibran's wisdom as my manifesto.

be still

On Children

Your children are not your children.

They are the sons and daughters of Life's longing for itself.

They come through you but not from you,

And though they are with you, yet they belong not to you.

You may give them your love but not your thoughts.

For they have their own thoughts.

You may house their bodies but not their souls,

For their souls dwell in the house of tomorrow,

which you cannot visit, not even in your dreams.

~Kahlil Gibran

How profound. Just like the saying, "Give them roots and give them wings." That's what I would want to do. I secretly always thought I would be an awesome mom someday, even though I wasn't sure I wanted to step into that arena.

I ended up having three kids in just over 3 years. I had no idea how complex and all-consuming it would be. The years went by and I think I was growing up right along side of them, trying to let go but not doing it, trying to let them live their own lives but not doing it, trying to accept that they are whole and good and capable without me lurking over their every move and managing their every thought, but not doing it. How oppressive! No wonder teenagers want to run away. I wanted to fix them and they weren't even broken. I was missing the everyday moments in anticipation of the amazing moments, when really the most ordinary moments are a perfect opportunity to see beauty and share love.

Thanks to my kids, I started to get it. It happened in one quick week, as if it were a vast left-wing conspiracy. My kids were still young, but each told me in their own way that they liked themselves just the way there are, and did not want to be molded into someone who we wanted them to be. They did not want to over-schedule themselves to the point of stress and anxiety. They did not want to kiss up to their teachers for good grades. They did not want to make every decision based on getting into college. In a nutshell, they did not want us packaging their lives, or planning their future. Or their present.

Even though their words were not quite that direct, that's what I heard. And they were right. I needed to be sure they were safe and their basic needs were met, but we had gotten caught up in the crazy whirlwind of modern-day high school, where the robbers of joy have invaded campuses and houses everywhere. Fun and joy were replaced with churning out high-achieving kids, where good character, confidence, joy and kindness are irrelevant compared to AP classes, GPA's and SAT scores. We fortunately found a school that honors and encourages art, music, character, critical thinking and values. And we shifted in our home, too.

So that's it. It's far from perfect, but I've mostly stepped off the hamster wheel. Most days I'm not spinning through the high school years like a drill sergeant, although the kids may disagree, especially during finals. Philosophically, I am trying to make my way back to Gibran. I am trying to step aside and give my children a gift, which is really their right, one that I had sadly taken away many years ago.

You see, I was treating them like bread dough. At first I mixed all the ingredients and then I kneaded it and kneaded it until it was the right consistency. Then, just as it started to rise, I pounded it down and covered it up until it started to rise again. And then I repeated that, over and over again. But now I see a different path. Kids need space to rise and grow and fill the corners of the room with their beings. So now in our house the dough is rising and forming and discovering it's own fullness and air pockets and spaces to fill. And when it works, it is beautiful.

I am so grateful for this change of direction. As I told my kids, "I am so sorry for the times you felt like you were living life in a pressure cooker. You are free. Free to explore, free to make mistakes, free to discover the dreams you have for yourself, not the dreams that we have chosen for you."

Ha! I sound so evolved. But I'm so full of it. I did deliver that deep and profoundly thoughtful speech to them, but I'm pretty sure that within a half an hour I was biting my tongue before I launched uncontrollably into my daily checklist of questions. The truth is, I have a lot of work to do. It's hard to watch them fail, or be lazy. I've come a long way in letting go, and it does appear to me that the less I do, the more they can do. I still get a little nervous about high school and college stuff, and won't tolerate a lack of kindness or compassion. But in the back of my mind I am aware that they have their own journey and they are good people. They are writing their own story. And I should step aside and let them grow.

Thank you Kahlil Gibran, because truly I want them to know that I love them just the way they are, that they belong here and are always welcome just as they are. I will be here to house their bodies, but not their souls.

Show Up and Finish Well

CHAPTER 9

Showing Up With Charity and Contribution

Live deeply. Deeply within.

Where your ageless soul
  greets your gentle knowing heart.
Listen in stillness,
  for wisdom and truth reside here.

But live deeply on the outside, too.
Where your light shines
  and your love is made visible.

Where your heart moves to the rhythm
of pure and honest care
for your fellow man.

Because truly this entire planet
is but one heart, beating in unison.

~ Diane R. Button

The Research About Charity and Contribution

As we reach the end of our lives and look back, it is clear that the people who we know and love are the most meaningful, important, tangible parts of our lives. We want to have loved. And we want to have been loved. But there is another equally dynamic and relevant aspect of life that people consistently site as a major component of a meaningful life. It is often expressed in hospice as a question.

"Did my life matter?"

"Did I make a difference?"

"Will I be remembered for how I served others?"

 "Is the world a better place because I was here?"

The common thread is that people want to have given more than they have taken. They were not necessarily looking to save the world or to be known for their heroic acts. In a more simple way, they wanted to be sure that they made a contribution that helped make the world a better place. Like their children and grandchildren, this imprint on the world is part of their legacy. And they want to finish well.

Purpose in life is closely linked to charity, service and giving. In his book, *The 10 Secrets of Success and Inner*

Peace, the late Dr. Wayne Dyer urges people to find their passion by "listening to your own music" to discover our own unique purpose in life. He believes that a person will not find inner peace if they do not know why they are here and what they are supposed to be doing with their precious time on this planet. Dr. Dyer believes that purpose is always about serving. He writes, "You come into this world with absolutely nothing. You will leave this physical world with exactly the same. All of your acquisitions and achievements can't go with you. Therefore, the only thing you can do with your life is give it away. You'll find yourself feeling purposeful if you can find a way to always be in the service of others (Dyer, 2001, p. 45)."

Another leader in the field of mind-body medicine and human potential is Deepak Chopra, author of *The Seven Spiritual Laws of Success*. One of the laws involves "dharma" which implies that each person has a unique talent and means for expression of their talents, that match up through the miracle of our existence with a unique need in the universe. The three components of his law of Dharma are: We are each here to discover our true and spiritual Self; we are here to discover our unique talent; and we are here to serve our fellow human beings. Dr. Chopra simplifies these components by describing that the ego tends to ask "What's in it for me?" but the spiritual self would ask instead, "How can I help?" Ultimately, according to Dr. Chopra, our purpose in life will be revealed when we learn how we can serve humanity.

Victor Frankl noted in *Man's Search for Meaning* that success, similar to happiness, occurs in a person's life only as a by-product of dedicating one's life to a cause greater than oneself. When Frankl's original manuscript was confiscated in Auschwitz, he began writing down bits and pieces of information on pieces of scrap paper. His motivation to share his information and make a contribution to others was a driving force in his desire and will to live. He once said, "Only to the extent that someone is living out this self-transcendence of human existence, is he truly human or does he become his true self. He becomes so, not by concerning himself with his self's actualization, but by forgetting himself and giving himself, overlooking himself and focusing outward."

There have been many famous quotes and speeches about the benefits and rewards of charity, contribution, giving and striving to make the world better place. Albert Schweitzer said, "I don't know what your destiny will be, but one thing I do know: the only ones among you who will be really happy are those who have sought and found how to serve." The Buddha said, "If you knew what I know about the power of giving, you would not let a single meal pass without sharing it in some way." And Deepak Chopra said, "Everyone has a purpose in life … a unique gift or special talent to give to others. And when we blend this unique talent with service to others, we experience the ecstasy and exultation of our own spirit, which is the ultimate goal of all goals."

Every person I have interviewed was motivated to give their time and energy to causes that benefit others. Some participants noted that the world is a different and more complex place than it was back when they were younger, and part of their contribution involves paying attention to these changes. For example, along with volunteering for organizations or working in the helping profession, many now share a concern and an interest in protecting the planet and the environment even if it is done in simple ways, like voting or recycling. Contribution was viewed as both an obligation and a privilege. At this later stage in life, people are pondering what their life on earth has meant and whether or not they made a difference.

In my interviews, the topic that generated the most profound thoughts from people in the final stage of their life was that of charity and contribution. Overall, there was a deep, heartfelt, and honest desire to leave the world a better place because they were here. They wanted to believe that their time here on earth was meaningful, not only to themselves, but to a greater whole. That was achieved in a variety of ways including protecting the planet and the environment, volunteering with the Peace Corps or at church, participating in their local community, coaching, raising kids, being kind to others, teaching, giving time and energy to others, listening to and caring for those in need, counseling, opening their home for others to enjoy, sharing food, and more. Not one person mentioned money. The results have suggested that it is not money or material possessions that contribute to happiness or have anything to do with personal fulfillment. Joy and happiness appear to come from within and cannot be seen, and the greatest and most meaningful, lasting sense of joy comes from serving others.

Stories about Charity and Contribution

A Whopper of a Day

At the end of life we will not be judged by how many diplomas we have earned, how much money is in our bank account, or how many grand things we have done. If we were to be judged at all, it should be because of how we treated one another. Did we feed the hungry and the homeless, did we give clothes to those in need? Mother Teresa taught us all about giving as a sacrifice. She encouraged us all to stretch beyond our comfort zones. She says, "I ask you one thing: do not tire of giving, but do not give your leftovers. Give until it hurts, until you feel the pain." I have heard some say that, when you feel the pain in your pocketbooks, you will soon feel the joy in your heart. Give abundantly of your time, money, energy, and love.

Mother Teresa also taught us that, while we are all called to serve others, we must also remember to tread with care so as to not rob those we serve of their pride, their self-esteem or their dignity. I remembered this with a recent hospice patient. This woman looked brittle and weak and the cancer was ravaging her body, but I also saw a strong, proud, independent German woman trapped inside her failing body. My task for the day was to take her to the Department of Motor Vehicles to get a State ID card, since her driver's license and passport had both expired. It meant a lot to this woman to have a valid identity, and I was going to make sure she got one!

With help from the nurses, we got her into my car and off we went. She did not answer my questions or speak to me in the car. She was clearly uncomfortable about being out with a stranger and did not want to talk. I respected that, and I remained quiet. We got to the building and a strong young man helped me get her out of the car and into her wheelchair. She sat clinging to her box of documents, which the nurses assured me were all in order and complete.

At the window inside the Department of Motor Vehicles we were greeted by a surly, apparently over-worked woman. She seemed to enjoy heartlessly rejecting customers, one after another. We heard her tell everyone in front of us that they needed to come back some other time. Then it was our turn. The uptight cashier reviewed the documents and told my hospice patient that the documents she brought were not enough and that we needed to leave and come back another day. Well, there was no way in hell I was leaving there without that woman's State ID card.

I didn't want to take over, but I knew this meant a lot to her, so I asked if I could help by looking in her box for some other valid document. We didn't want to lose our place in line, so I started handing my hospice patient cards that we knew wouldn't work, like a library card or a receipt from the grocery store. She understood the game plan immediately. She gently and slowly handed each one to Surly, buying a little more time, as I kept digging for some other proof of ID to use. We became a team. The woman was not going to give up and neither was I. After what seemed like an eternity, just as I was getting to the bottom of the documents files, I saw an old Medicare statement with her home address on it. Hallelujah! We did it! Too bad, Surly Uptight Person! I think we ruined her winning streak. The packet was stamped abruptly and we were told to go into the waiting room until they called her name for a photo.

At that point we realized that everyone in the waiting room had been watching us and silently cheering us on. My hospice patient started talking to me and showing me the photos in her birth certificate, which was like an elegant book, from Germany. She came alive, recounting stories about the war and her childhood. Soon the entire waiting room was involved, smiling, laughing and listening with admiration as the woman shared about her history and her heritage.

After a few minutes, they called her name and I wheeled her up to the window for her photo. The crowd cheered out loud for her and she perked up, like she had just consumed a giant Monster drink. When the cashier from the DMV told her to smile, the woman grinned from ear to ear with a gigantic smile that lit up the entire room. It occurred to me that this might be the last photo ever taken of her. And she was smiling.

I had already arranged for a strapping, handsome Tongan man we met in the waiting room to help me get her back into the car, and that made her smile once again. This time, when we started driving home, she could not stop talking. She was so excited about her ID, and the wonderful people she met in the waiting room, and the kind men who helped her in and out of the car. She saw goodness in humanity that day. She got out of the house for a while, and she felt like she had accomplished something. I helped her, but she did it. I was just on her team. I try to only jump in when I'm needed with Hospice patients because I know that simple freedoms and independence are often being taken away from them, bit by bit.

She was so excited in the car she said, "Wow, what a day! I don't know about you, but I'm starving. Can I buy you lunch?"

"I'm not too hungry right now, but I'll get something to drink. Let's do it. Where do you want to go?" I asked.

"Can we go to Burger King? I love Burger King and I haven't been there in years and years."

I'm not use to hearing that from Hospice patients so I called the nurse just to make sure it was OK for her to eat fast food. It was approved, so off we went to Burger King. I asked her if she wanted me to go in and order or drive thru. "Let's drive thru," she said. She even told me which parking spot she wanted to park in after, so she could have a view of the majestic mountains while she ate her lunch.

We pulled up to the drive thru and, in the spirit of fostering her independence, I suggested that she tell the voice coming from the box what she wanted for lunch. She leaned in front of me towards the box and said with a strong, self-assured German accent, "I'll have 2 Whoppers, please." She looked at me, winked, and smiled that same giant smile I saw earlier. Then we both burst out laughing. Oh yes, what a day!

Marian Wright Edelman said, "We must not, in trying to think about how we can make a big difference, ignore the small daily differences we can make which, over time, add up to big differences that we often cannot foresee." This reminds me of Mother Teresa's urging us all to do small things with great love, and the simple recording of the life of Jesus, encapsulated in Acts 10:38 which says that Jesus "went about doing good."

I love Mother Teresa's story about a Hindu family with eight children who were very hungry. A concerned man came to see Mother Teresa and told her about the family. Mother Teresa immediately gathered enough rice for a meal and went to their home, where she saw all the hungry faces. The mother took the rice, divided it in half and left the house.

When she returned Mother Teresa asked her, "Where did you go?"

It turns out the woman had gone to her next-door neighbors house, a Muslim family, also with eight children. She said to Mother Teresa, "They are also hungry." This mother had the courage and the generosity of spirit to share half the rice with her neighbors, even though her own family was very hungry. Mother Teresa knew this made the woman feel good to be able to share.

Because she wanted to make sure the woman felt happy for her goodness, Mother Teresa did not go back and bring more rice to the woman for her own family. She waited until the following day.

be still

Money is captivating. When one is lifted up to the penthouse, passing by the poor or less financially fortunate, it is easy to lose your real sense of purpose. If it is true that the more you have been given, the more you shall be expected to give, then this is a call to love and care for others in a way that could lead us to live in a much more balanced world. Why are so many people starving while others are regularly dining on lobster and caviar? If blessed with abundance, let your character be one of generosity and contribution. If not, it can be lonely at the top. Remember the hungry, the homeless, the poor, the imprisoned, those in need and remember your neighbor. Make a difference to just one person and you will change the world.

But money is not the only path to charity and contribution. Service comes in many forms, and true service is never motivated by profit or applause. Some will tirelessly labor in support of others. Some will grow crops or build schools and shelters. Some will give counsel or, as is with Hospice, some may simply sit quietly at the bedside of a terminally ill patient.

Some serve others with encouragement. If your light is bright enough, you can help another person to polish away the tarnished, scratched and bruised exterior so that the gem that is their heart and soul can shine again.

Some serve because they have a dream that is burning inside their soul. Touring the Civil Rights Museum in Memphis our kids learned about one of the most passionate dreamers the world has ever known, Dr. Martin Luther King, Jr. He lived his dream until his death and shared his dream on the steps of the Lincoln Memorial in front of thousands of people. My kids learned one sentence that day that would forever change how they viewed themselves as part of a bigger whole of humanity. I am forever grateful for that lesson, and that day. Their eyes were glued to the old-style black and white TV screen, where they heard Dr. King speak with unforgettable conviction, passion and hope for a better tomorrow. He said, "I have a dream that my four children will one day live in a nation where they will not be judged by the color of their skin, but by the content of their character. I have a dream today."

I owe a sincere thank you to Dr. King and his famous speech, because his dream rubbed off on my young children that day. I won't do the mommy brag thing, but because my kids learned to care about the content of their character, they care about others. Because they care about others, they have already made the entire world a better place. We can all do this. And we can all teach our children well.

A few more words by Dr. King: "Everybody can be great...because anybody can serve. You don't have to have a college degree to serve. You don't have to make your subject and verb agree to serve. You only need a heart full of grace. A soul generated by love."

Favorite Quotes on Our Refrigerator

We make a living by what we get.

We make a life by what we give.

~Winston Churchill

This one is worth repeating:

"I don't know what your destiny will be, but one thing I do know: the only ones among you who will be really happy are those who have sought and found how to serve."

~Albert Schweitzer

The fruit of silence is prayer

The fruit of prayer is faith

The fruit of faith is love

The fruit of love is service

The fruit of service is peace.

~Anonymous

I slept and dreamt that life was joy.

I awoke and saw that life was service.

I acted and behold,

service was joy.

~ Rabindranath Tagore

be still

Mark suggested a few months ago that I get some help in the house on a regular basis. That way I could actually focus on my writing and also have the foot surgery that I have been dreading, and therefore avoiding. At first I felt I didn't deserve the extra help. Thankfully the loving voice of my higher power told the naggy, mean, controlling, inner voice sitting on my right shoulder to shut the hell up and let me have some space and time to follow my dreams. So I called Connie.

Connie is a neighbor who I have known for years, but not that well. She is kind, spiritual, and very low-key. She's been through a lot so she is wise and sensitive and I love having her energy in my house. She always walks in with this vibe, like His Holiness the Dalai Lama was waiting for her on my porch and gave her a personal blessing of peace before she walked through my front door.

Soon I noticed that each time she left my house there was a little bag of chocolate graham crackers or a few oranges or some lilikoi fruits on my counter, but I never knew where they came from. I thought maybe she dug them up from under my kid's bed or Mark left them there. Then one day Connie came to clean my house with her daughter and they brought me a beautiful bunch of bird of paradise flowers from their yard. It dawned on me that all those other "offerings" may also be coming from her. So I paid attention.

As the weeks went by she left me books to borrow, little packets of eye drops for my dry eyes, more fruits, an oregano plant and once she even left me a small, plastic bag with two taro root dinner rolls. This reminded me of the incense and candle offerings that sit in the back corner of our local nail salon, along with a random coke and an apple or a tangerine. One time I saw the plate in the nail salon filled with skittles and two whole walnuts. I learned that, in Buddhism, the incense, flowers, food and drink offerings represent devoting all of a person's senses to their spiritual practice.

I don't know if Connie is Buddhist, and that doesn't matter to me. What matters is that Connie reminds me to serve. But more than that, she reminds me to serve in silence, without ego, expecting nothing in return. I have a long way to go, but I still pay attention. And I feel honored to have Connie come into my home.

Showing Up with Humility

I want so much to be humble. My heart wants to give and give and give with no expectation and no need for accolades. My intentions are good, but then every once in awhile the all-consuming egomaniac comes exploding out of me like an air bag, taking over every possible inch of space and goodness and humility. Damn ego.

My grandfather was the epitome of humble. I would often hear stories about him and see articles in medical journals and magazines about his work as a plastic surgeon specializing in burns, but he never talked about it with us. He and my grandmother lived in San Francisco and I used to drive across the Golden Gate Bridge to visit them on weekends. I always tried to get them to tell me stories about all the wonderful things my grandfather did. He would usually start out talking about a "case" and just when I thought I would hear some amazing story about how he saved someone's life, he would talk about how amazing the patient was and what they had done that touched my grandfather so deeply. I know he saved lots of lives because I have met many people

216

who have told me, "Your grandfather is an amazing man. He saved my life." Or "my husband's life." Or "my brother's life."

One dreary wet Saturday afternoon my grandmother and I went down to the local market to get some food for dinner. My grandmother was perusing the canned corn when I quietly stepped away to find some fresh corn in the produce section. Suddenly I heard a very loud and excited voice saying, "Oh my God, Rosemary, I am so happy to see you! My son is so healthy and alive and is living a full and complete life. And I owe it all to the Good Doctor. He saved my son's life."

By now I was back with my grandmother and the canned corn, staring at a beautiful woman with tears streaming uncontrollably down her face.

"This is my granddaughter, Diane," my grandmother said. I'm sure she was hoping the beautiful, well-dressed woman would not notice my "hippy" braids, bandana, beads and colorful outfit, but I could tell this woman could not have cared less what I looked like. She grabbed me and hugged me for a long time, like she was sending me a telepathic message that had to find it's way through our clothes and purses and stuff. She was not letting go until she felt like I got it. And I got it. She was overcome with gratitude. She had a full, thankful heart.

She pulled back, still holding my arms and asked, "Do you have any idea what your grandfather did for my son?"

"No, I'm sorry, I don't know. But tell me."

Through tears she said, "My son was born with a rare medical abnormality. His future looked bleak and we were told he might have to live his life in some sort of a protective shell, at least until he was full-grown. We were devastated and scared, and we had no money. But then we heard about the Good Doctor. We called and told him we had no money, and he kindly agreed to see us anyway."

She paused, "That in itself was a blessing, that the Good Doctor was willing to see us, but do you know what your grandfather did for my little boy?"

This was awesome as I was getting to hear a real life story about the man I respected more than anyone else I had ever met. "No, tell me more. What did he do?"

"He healed my son and stayed committed to him for years. After your grandfather operated on him, my son was able to go outside and live his life. And not only that, as he grew the Good Doctor operated on him over and over again, until he was an adult and able to have a more permanent procedure that would last for years to come. Your grandfather is the most humble, giving man I have ever known."

"I know he is," I said, bursting with joy. The woman hugged me again because there was still a lot of gratitude inside her that she wanted to share. She even wiggled a bit because there was just no way she could express it all. But I got it.

The woman left, still crying. And I was crying, too. I looked at my 80-pound grandmother and she wasn't crying or even very emotional. She was just grinning with pride, but ready to get on with her day.

"How come you're not all crying and gushy like me?" I asked her.

She replied simply, "I love hearing these stories. It warms my heart, but it doesn't make me cry anymore because, the truth is, I hear them all the time."

Oh my. What a pure, full, honest and complete life.

I went home and cuddled next to him, so grateful to be part of this family and just hoping that the tiniest bit of his humility and goodness would rub off on me.

CHAPTER 10

The Final Chapter

My Eulogy

Only when you drink from the river of silence shall you indeed sing.

And when you have reached the mountain top, then you shall begin to climb.

And when the earth shall claim your limbs, then shall you truly dance.

~ Kahlil Gibran

Opening Song: by Lynyrd Skynyrd
"Freebird"

If I leave here tomorrow

Would you still remember me?

For I must be traveling on now

'Cause there's too many places I've got to see...

be still

Love is Ridiculous

By Hannah Button – age 15

March 7, 2015

My mom, being the spiritual and deep-thinking person she is, thinks a lot about death as well as love. Another quality she has that is honestly one of my least favorites is that she never likes to be a burden on anyone, so she does everything she can to take care of herself and everyone else around her. Examples include but are not limited to: walking around two days after foot surgery so she could cook for her family, or helping us to run a garage sale while sick from chemo, and even writing her own eulogy so her family wouldn't be "burdened" with doing it ourselves. Ridiculous!

Naturally, an obvious option for the person chosen to read my mom's eulogy would be my dad, her husband of 18 years. But being the weird person my dad is, he refused to be the one to read off my mother's last and most profound sentiments, the legacy she wanted to leave behind after her soul had left this world. He simply stated that they have a "deal" that he was "supposed to die first." Also ridiculous.

Some might call that statement uncaring, depressing, or stony-hearted, but I am related to those idiots, and to me it isn't any of those things. It's beautiful, profound, but most of all, real love. He's not saying he wants to die first, he's saying he would rather have her be alive than him. He isn't saying that he doesn't care about his life, he's saying that she is the part of his life that means the most to him, but above all else, he is saying that he would rather be dead than have to spend a day without her by his side.

Love is ridiculous. It makes us do or say things that are stupid, or horrible, or profound, and everything in between. Don't get me wrong, I ain't no love expert, I am fifteen years old and haven't been on a date, let alone experienced that kind of love, but I know that my parents love each other enough that all the stupid, horrible, and profound stuff is worth it in every way, because that's what love is.

Ridiculous, but perfect.

My Eulogy

Seems a little odd, I know. Why on earth would I want to spend my days writing my own eulogy? I just think it's a hard job to leave for a grieving family, and besides, no one knows me better than I know myself.

This eulogy will be short, but real. It will be true and deep and honest. It may even be funny, although I make no guarantees at this early stage. It will almost certainly NOT be filled with fluffy, generic, homogenous or embellished adjectives designed to make me look as if the world's first perfect person just left the planet. I know some people love me and will miss me, but I know myself better than even you. I was far from perfect.

This eulogy, considering that it is mine, would be absolutely incomplete without some opportunities for all of you, who are still stuck here to pay taxes and wash dishes, to learn some of the tidbits I have gathered along the way about making this the most meaningful life you could ever live.

But first, let's talk about me. I think I was an exceptional, out-of-the-box, and very loving mom. I was an irritating, lovable wife who drove her husband crazy with her desire to have every molecule of air that the entire family breathed broken down into pre-specified pouches with perfect instructions explained in thorough detail. Yes, I was a planner. And as a friend, I was direct, nurturing and everyone knew that they could count on me. If I said I was going to do something, it would be done...early.

Other than that, I was just a normal, everyday person, trying to get by in life. Maybe I was able to help someone else from time to time or do something rewarding, but mostly I was just putting one foot in front of the other and hoping to make it to some undefined, ever-changing, and elusive successful place. Probably just like you.

I am sorry that I used so many plastic bottles. I am sorry that I may not have returned your phone call or responded to your email. I am sorry that I forgot your birthday. My kids told someone once that we do not recycle and that is not true. They lied. We recycle. But we could have definitely done a better job and I am sorry for that, too.

Also, if you ever stayed at my house and you were one of my healthy friends, I probably hid a diet coke or some jellybeans from you. I would have shared them but I know they were not good for me and, as much as I love you, I didn't want to hear about it. They were usually in my top dresser drawer. At Easter they were the standard jellybeans. The rest of the year they were Jelly Belly. Occasionally, there were also Red Vines. I'm sorry for being sneaky.

It has always been a priority for me to teach and build up my kids so that they and their generation could rise up and change the world. I hope I have brought a few of their friends along, too. I thought childbirth was a beautiful thing, but I was not about to waste all of that pain and the loss of my sexy figure on yucky kids. I made some mistakes and lost my temper at times, but I pray that they all know that I tried my very best and that what mattered was that they knew they were loved.

Seeking Joy

Fond memories have always carried me through. Thank you all for the laughter and the joy. It seems to me that sometimes it's easier to sit and wallow in the hard stuff than to truly experience joy. Maybe it's because we are afraid the joy will pass and so we had better not get too comfortable with all those good feelings! That's ridiculous! Embrace joy. It took me a long time to get there. The deal is, when sad times come, you are going to get sad anyway. So when joy comes, feel that, too.

I find that so much of my joy has come from the simple little everyday memories. For example, on 11/11/2011 our entire family ran into the ocean and at exactly 11:11am we were all holding our breath underwater. It was a 30 second memory, but I will guess that we were the only family in the entire world who were all underwater intentionally holding our breath on 11/11/11 at 11:11am. And just in case some other family had the same idea, we were also all eating a grape. It's the little things that have given me the greatest joy.

All of us going under water at 11/11/11 at 11:11 am.

Joy comes from remembering when Jack used to lick the screen door because he liked the taste of salt. Or when Hannah caught a firefly and named her Annabelle. And then how the firefly got away and when Hannah caught another one she came running into the kitchen with her bouncing blonde hair, screeching with delight, "Look Mommy, I found

Annabelle!" Joy comes when Carly hugs a sick orphaned boy named Moses and I know her heart is all in.

Joy comes when your mom waters your friend's marijuana plants after work every day, thinking it is just his garden, and she takes it so seriously that she leaves work early to make sure she does a good job. Thanks, mom.

Sometimes joy even comes in the hard stuff. One time I took Jack on a winter bonding trip to Crested Butte, Colorado. It was a beautiful week, and we were on the last ski run of the day. Jack wanted to show me all that he had learned. He was doing great until he fell down, tired from a long day. I put out a hand to help him up, but instead I fell on top of him. I wish I could say that we both cracked up laughing, but that is not what happened. What happened was that I snapped his tibia right in two. I felt terrible, but he was such a loving angel. He told me over and over again that he forgave me for breaking his "amphibian bone." The funniest part was that he called his grandma and told her that I had broken his amphibian bone, and she called all the rest of the family and all her friends and told them all that I broke Jack's amphibian bone, too. Oh, joy! But that's our story and ours alone. What are your stories? Share them, for they let people in.

Rather than spending so much time seeking money, fame, success, and glory, simply seek joy, for joy is the song of your heart. Make new stories. Cultivate joy now. Express gratitude now. Live your dreams now. Don't wait for someone to die, or the cancer diagnosis, or the car accident. Be smarter than that. Be the one who doesn't need the massive wake-up call to wake up!

However joy comes, let it come!

Togetherness

If I were there, I would invite you all over to my house at the same time. We would all cuddle up like a bunch of newborn puppies. I would see YOU in your eyes, in your words and in the connection between you and me and all of us. I would remind you what you have added to my life, what I learned from you and I would tell you why I love you.

God did not create any of us to be superior or better than anyone else. There is not one person alive who knows all things, nor is there one person alive who does not know at least one thing that you do not know. What that means is that there is something you can learn from every person. Look to your right, and to your left. We are all teachers. My son is my teacher. My friend is my teacher and my enemy is, too. The clerk in the grocery store is my teacher and you are my teacher. Embrace every person as if they were bringing a fragile gift to you…something that you do not have.

Live a Simple Life

Peel away the glitter and the bling.

Remove your eye make-up and your fancy shoes.

Step off your thrones and discard your titles.

Throw away your labels and "what you do."

Forget about your street address or your zip code.

Say goodbye to all that tethers and ties you to your ego

Like the grandiose strings of a puppeteer.

Remove the veil for you are none of that.

You are that which remains.

And that miracle is the essence of your soul.

For some unexplainable reason, it has almost always

been important to me that I am prepared and ready to die. Sometimes my drawers are not as tidy as I would like, so I may be slightly embarrassed when one of you cleans out my room. And I may have forgotten to get a bikini wax or to shave my legs, but I trust that whoever cares for my body after my death is also not a perfect person. My request is that you treat me with love and respect and don't laugh at any of the body parts that I have stupidly spent a lifetime trying to hide from you and everyone else.

In general, this day will not hit me by surprise. I live with a profound awareness that my next breath is not guaranteed. It is my extremely unprofessional opinion that accepting the inevitability of death brings more joy, gratitude, love, awareness and presence to our every day life. It opens the heart. It reveals who, and what, we want to keep close to our hearts, and what we are willing to let go of. I look at life like a short vacation with a small suitcase...carry-on only. There's not a lot of room for excess, so only pack what you really want and need. Sitting with dying people has helped me to accept that it will someday be my turn. And I want to be ready. And if I get the chance, I will hold all of my children and look deeply into my husband's eyes every day until that day comes. Just because.

I've tried not to carry around unfinished business. If I have not reached out to you to bring closure to an open wound, then it was not intended to hurt you. It was intended to protect me. I may not be very outwardly gushy and demonstrative like some of my girlfriends who kiss you on the lips like adorable golden retrievers, but I sure hope you know that I loved you. The years have made me tender and have broken my heart wide open.

You all know about "The 7 Components of a Meaningful Life" and how they have impacted how I lived my own life. Today is beautiful, but what will you do with your tomorrow? What will you do when this moment is over? I encourage you to look fearlessly towards your future. Imagine yourself getting old. Imagine your hands and your body, your face and your hair. Imagine your heart and imagine that you are feeling the joy, peace and love that all comes from living a meaningful life.

Do not be afraid to ask yourself what is keeping you from joy. Or what is keeping you from peace? Is there anyone who you have not forgiven or apologized to? Or anyone who you have not loved well? Now is the time to make amends so you can start each day with a clean, white slate.

I pray fervently that I have not taken anyone for granted. My soul departs with love for all beings and an understanding of my connectedness to the divine. And I am acutely aware of my connection to all of you. You who held my hand, suffered with me or cried with me. You who laughed with me, challenged me, cheered for me, and played with me. You who shared soup with me last week and you who share memories with me from days long past. I love you all. I am also aware of my connection to the trees that rise towards the heavens, and my ancestors whose dirty, calloused hands planted seeds in the fertile soil generations ago. I am aware of my connection to those who bent over in the fields to pick the fruit that ended up on my table, those whose rugged hands voyaged into unchartered lands in hopes of a better life, and those skilled laborers who sewed the fabrics together to make the shirts that have covered my back from the afternoon sun. I thank you all. We truly are one heart beating in unison, the great pulse of our planet earth.

Closing Song by Mercy Me
"I Can Only Imagine"

I can only imagine what it will be like
When I walk by Your side
I can only imagine what my eyes will see
When Your face is before me…

Surrounded by Your glory
What will my heart feel?
Will I dance for You Jesus?
Or in awe of You be still?....

Will I stand in Your presence
To my knees will I fall?
Will I sing, Hallelujah?
Will I be able to speak at all?
I can only imagine...

Well Done

I will close with this. There are 3 scriptures that have guided my life and, when combined, encompass all the seven components of a meaningful life. I hope to have passed mercifully and peacefully, surrounded by love, with these same words ringing truth in my ears as I took my final breath.

Number 1: "Be still and know that I am God." Psalm 46:10

In everyday life, this was the moment-to-moment, day-by-day, year-by-year call from my soul. Be still. It is about trusting God, pausing, praying and listening to the sweet sound of silence rather than always being busy. It includes **gratitude**, **acceptance**, and living with a healthy and **positive attitude**. This was the internal mantra of my life.

Number 2: "He went about doing good." Acts 10:38

This was the external living, walking mantra of my life. It is about living a life that glorifies God, which to me meant trying to do what Jesus would do. It was about living a life of **intention**, with a focus on the importance of **love and relationships**, and **charity and contribution**. It was about waking up every morning and asking myself, "Who can I serve today?"

Number 3: "Well done good and faithful servant." Matthew 25:21

This bible verse reminds me that life is designed to prepare us all for something greater. It is reflective and, for me, it is about **faith and spirituality**, but in the context of how we lived and chose to use what we were given, whether it is talent, money, time, strength, opportunities or knowledge. It is about finishing well.

It takes all the seven components of a meaningful life to truly and wholeheartedly show up for life. This was the goal that motivated me every morning to get up and start again. Until the end, every day was a new opportunity to show up and finish well.

I hope I showed up for you. Thank you for showing up for me.

This will be my final goodbye. I pray that you know that I heard you. I saw you. And I valued you. You made my life have meaning and you mattered to me. You matter to the world. You are a child of God and you are my friend. I am eternally grateful for your fingerprints that touched my soul, and for your footprints that walked by my side.

With indescribable peace, gratitude, love and contentment,

Diane

Acknowledgements

"There is no JOY without gratitude."

- Brene Brown

This book would not have been possible without the history of friends and family members who have brought boundless joy, deep suffering, honesty, and hilarious stories into my every day life.

Thank you to my editor and contributor, Hannah Lee Kealoha Button, for your dedication to this project. Your insight, vocabulary, depth, and creativity has expanded, stretched and improved this book. You are one special human.

Thank you, Mark, for the countless hours you have showed up for me, not just for this project, but also for the last 20 years. Thank you for your input, your tech skills, your patience, your ideas, and your guidance with this book. I love you and how we blend together so well.

Thank you to my mentor and Goddard College professor, Dr. Jim Fitzgerald. You gave me encouragement and inspired me to hold this project close to my heart, yet to share it with the world. I am forever grateful to you, to Dr. Tracy Garrett, and to my other Goddard professors. In addition, thank you

Maryellen McCone and fellow students, for sharing this journey with me.

Thank you to Hospice Hawaii, especially Clarence Liu, and all hospice patients and families who have given me the privilege of sitting by your side and listening to your stories. You have touched me deeply and, in death, have taught me so much about life.

Thank you to those who allowed me to interview them for the research portion of this book, especially Sylvia and Seymour Boorstein, who are role models to many of us when it comes to exploring and living a meaningful life. Each of you gave me your all and provided the foundations of the 7 components of a meaningful life.

Thank you to all of you whose personal stories are included in these pages, and all of you who encouraged me so much along the way, including Hannes Arch and Miriam, Kathy Altz, Liz Boorstein, Paul and Karen Burrous, Collette Cameron, Cathy Capper, Peter Carter, Reggie Casadei, Debrah Farentino, Connie Froemsdorf, Jimmy Gentry, Becky Lile, Kendra Martyn, Tom Mitchell, Michelle Mykeloff, Carlos Omphroy, Theresa Parisher, Dr. Fred Peipman, Twila Richvalsky, Nancy Thomas, Emily Wikman, and Victor from San Miguel de Allende. You, along with the rest of my tribe, all keep me healthy and unafraid to follow my dreams.

I am forever grateful for our deep and wide circle of friends. I know that I am very fortunate to have understood early on that love and relationships are one of life's greatest keys to a meaningful life. You come from many cities, states, countries, and continents and I hope you know that, no matter how far away you are, I will always show up for you.

Thank you to my parents, Rosemary Steiss and Robert Renn, for believing in me. I would not be who I am today without you. And thank you for encouraging me to be brave enough to print more than just three copies of this book for my kids.

Thank you to my brother, Tony Renn, for teaching me that all things are possible and that a tiny sliver of light can indeed fill a dark space. You are my hero and I am proud of you.

Thank you to my extended family, including Orville and Pauline Button, Aunt Toni Alstad, Ann "Poppy" Devincenzi, Michelle Traenkner, Scott and Diane Stillinger, Frank and Linda Riolo, Kelsey Stillinger and Jeff Des Jarlais, Doug Stillinger, Robyn Stevens and Holly Stroth. You all mean the world to me.

Thank you to all who support the kids and their ongoing projects at their non-profit, Dream of a Better World (www.itsourturnnow.blogspot.com).

You are touching the future generations and making a difference.

Thank you to my kids, Carly, Jack and Hannah, for being "you" and allowing me to tell your stories and share this book, which started out just for you. You all fill my heart with more than I could have ever imagined or hoped for.

You all showed up. Let's finish well.

References

Baruch, Bernard M. "A Quote by Bernard M. Baruch." *Goodreads*. Goodreads, 01 Jan. 2007. Web. 16 Aug. 2016. <http://www.goodreads.com/quotes/865-be-who-you-are-and-say-what-you-feel-because>. Quote often attributed to Dr. Seuss.

Berk, Laura E. *Development through the Lifespan*. Boston, MA: Allyn and Bacon, 2007. Print.

Brown, Brené. *Daring Greatly: How the Courage to Be Vulnerable Transforms the Way We Live, Love, Parent, and Lead*. New York, NY: Gotham, 2012. Print.

Buddha, Gautama. "A Quote by Gautama Buddha." *Goodreads*. Goodreads, 01 Jan. 2007. Web. 16 Aug. 2016. <http://www.goodreads.com/quotes/103598-if-you-knew-what-i-know-about-the-power-of>.

Campbell, Joseph, and Bill D. Moyers. *The Power of Myth*. New York: Doubleday, 1988. Print.

Chopra, Deepak, and Deepak Chopra. *The Seven Spiritual Laws of Success: A Practical Guide to the Fulfillment of Your Dreams*. San Rafael, CA: Amber-Allen Pub., 1994. Print.

The Definition of Friend." *Dictionary.com*. Dictionary.com, n.d. Web. 16 Aug. 2016. <http://www.dictionary.com/browse/friend>.

Dyer, Wayne W. "You Can't Give Away What You Don't Have." *Dr. Wayne Dyer's 10 Secrets for Success and Inner Peace*. Carlsbad, CA: Hay House, 2001. 45. Print.

Einstein, Albert. "A Quote by Albert Einstein." *Goodreads*. Goodreads, 01 Jan. 2007. Web. 16 Aug. 2016. <http://www.goodreads.com/quotes/987-there-are-only-two-ways-to-live-your-life-one>.

Emmons, Robert A. *Thanks!: How the New Science of Gratitude Can Make You Happier.* Boston: Houghton Mifflin, 2007. Print.

Erikson, Erik H. *The Life Cycle Completed.* London: W.W. Norton &., 1998. Print.

Frankl, Viktor E. *Man's Search for Meaning.* Boston: Beacon, 2006. Print.

Freud, Sigmund. "A Quote by Sigmund Freud." *Goodreads.* Goodreads, 01 Jan. 2007. Web. 16 Aug. 2016. <http://www.goodreads.com/quotes/129743-love-and-work-are-the-cornerstones-of-our-humanness>.

Gandhi, Mahatma. "A Quote by Mahatma Gandhi." *Goodreads.* Goodreads, 01 Jan. 2007. Web. 16 Aug. 2016. <http://www.goodreads.com/quotes/32745-nobody-can-hurt-me-without-my-permission>.

Gentry, Jimmy, and Paul Clements. *An American Life.* Franklin, TN: Pleasantview, 2002. Print. For more information about Jimmy Gentry

Gibran, Kahlil. "On Children." *The Prophet.* New York: Knopf, 1952. N. pag. Print.

The Holy Bible: New International Version, Containing the Old Testament and the New Testament. Grand Rapids: Zondervan Bible, 1978. Print.

Kornfield, Jack. *The Wise Heart: A Guide to the Universal Teachings of Buddhist Psychology.* New York: Bantam, 2008. Print. For more information about Jack Kornfield

Kushner, Harold S. *Living a Life That Matters: Resolving the Conflict between Conscience and Success.* New York: A.A. Knopf, 2001. Print.

Lewis, J. J. "Marian Wright Edelman Quotes." *About.com Education.* About Education, n.d. Web. 16

Aug.2016.<http://womenshistory.about.com/od/quotes/a/marian_edelman.htm>.

McLeod, Saul. "Carl Rogers." *Simply Psychology*. N.p., 2007. Web. 16 Aug. 2016. <http://www.simplypsychology.org/carl-rogers.html>.

Mercy Me. *I Can Only Imagine ; Word of God Speak*. Curb Records, 2003. CD.

Mitchell, Joni. *Big Yellow Taxi*. Joni Mitchell. Reprise, 1995. CD.

Neal, Meghan. "I Have A Dream Speech (TEXT)." *The Huffington Post*. TheHuffingtonPost.com, 15 Jan. 2012. Web. 16 Aug. 2016. <http://www.huffingtonpost.com/2012/01/16/i-have-a-dream-speech-text-martin-luther-king-jr_n_1207734.html>.

Newport, Frank. "Religion." *Gallup.com*. Gallup, 3 June 2011. Web. 15 Aug. 2016. <http://www.gallup.com/poll/1690/Religion.aspx>.

Nietzsche, Friedrich. "Nietzsche Quotes." *Http://www.goodreads.com/quotes/137-he-who-has-a-why-to-live-for-can-bear*. Goodreads, 01 Jan. 2007. Web. 15 Aug. 2016.

O'Brien, Ron, Andy McKaie, and John Swenson. *Freebird*. Lynyrd Skynyrd. MCA Records, 1991. CD.

"A Quote by Sigmund Freud." *Goodreads*. Goodreads, 01 Jan. 2007. Web. 16 Aug. 2016. <http://www.goodreads.com/quotes/129743-love-and-work-are-the-cornerstones-of-our-humanness>.

Roosevelt, Eleanor. "A Quote by Eleanor Roosevelt." *Goodreads*. Goodreads, 01 Jan. 2007. Web. 16 Aug. 2016. <http://www.goodreads.com/quotes/569711-i-am-who-i-am-today-because-of-the-choices>.

Schweitzer, Albert. "A Quote by Albert Schweitzer." *Goodreads*. Goodreads, 01 Jan. 2007. Web. 16 Aug. 2016. <http://www.goodreads.com/quotes/74745-i-don-t-know-what-your-destiny-will-be-but-one>.

Shakespeare, William. "A Quote from Hamlet." *Goodreads*. Goodreads, 01 Jan. 2007. Web. 16 Aug. 2016. <http://www.goodreads.com/quotes/21959-there-is-nothing-either-good-or-bad-but-thinking-makes>.

Teresa, and José Luis. González-Balado. *Mother Teresa: In My Own Words*. New York: Gramercy, 1997. Print.

Thich Nhat Hanh. "A Quote by Thich Nhat Hanh." *Goodreads*. Goodreads, 01 Jan. 2007. Web. 15 Aug. 2016. <http://www.goodreads.com/quotes/5022-people-usually-consider-walking-on-water-or-in-thin-air>.

Ward, William A. "A Quote by William Arthur Ward." *Goodreads*. Goodreads, 01 Jan. 2007. Web. 16 Aug. 2016. <http://www.goodreads.com/quotes/189187-feeling-gratitude-and-not-expressing-it-is-like-wrapping-a>.

ABOUT THE AUTHOR

Diane is a successful entrepreneur, businesswoman and mother of three. She has a Masters in Counseling from Goddard College in Vermont and has published numerous articles. Her master's thesis, entitled *The 7 Components of a Meaningful Life*, became the genesis for *Show Up and Finish Well*. Along with her husband Mark, she co-authored *The Letter Box*, which recounts their triumph over tragedy and inspires others with a meaningful way to leave a legacy for those they love. Diane is the inspiration for and the Director of *"Dream of Better World,"* a non-profit, founded in 2008 with a two fold mission mission: to support disadvantaged children around the world, and; to inspire everyone to realize that *"You're never too young, or too old, to make a difference!"* In addition to her writing and non-profit work, Diane has spent many hours with hospice clients in their final days. She often refers to the insights gained from her research and from hospice clients when counseling others in finding purpose and direction in their lives.

Better World Publishing

58906579R00152

Made in the USA
Columbia, SC
27 May 2019